Why Y2K?

WHY Y2K?

What the millennium is really all about

John Blanchard

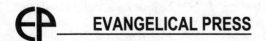

EVANGELICAL PRESS

EVANGELICAL PRESS
Grange Close, Faverdale North Industrial Estate, Darlington,
DL3 0PH, England

Evangelical Press USA
P. O. Box 84, Auburn, MA 01501, USA

e-mail : sales@evangelical-press.org
web : www.evangelical-press.org

First published 1999
Second impression 1999
Third impression 1999

British Library Cataloguing in Publication Data available

ISBN 0 85234 433 3

Other titles by John Blanchard

The Beatitudes for Today	Right with God
How to Enjoy your Bible	Truth for Life
Invitation to Live	Ultimate Questions
Luke Comes Alive!	Will the Real Jesus Please Stand Up?
Pop Goes the Gospel	What in the World is a Christian?
Read Mark Learn	Whatever Happened to Hell?

Printed and bound in Great Britain by Cox & Wyman Ltd, Reading

Contents

Introduction

It is safe to say that no single year in the history of the world has attracted more attention than the one which will begin on 1 January 2000. For the last decade, countries, communities and individuals have been making plans for the moment when 1999 becomes history and we enter a new millennium.

The time and money spent in planning the arrival of 2000 is literally beyond calculation and, as the birth of a new millennium is obviously a once-in-a-lifetime event for everybody, the determination to make it something which will never be forgotten mounts by the day.

Yet in all the frenzied planning, millions of people are ignoring the one question which everybody should be asking. The story is told of a prominent overseas dignitary who was to pay an official visit to one of Britain's leading public schools. As part of the preparation, a member of staff was assigned to show the visitor around, explain everything he would see, and highlight the most significant events in the school's history. For weeks beforehand, the teacher concerned did all he could to memorize the relevant facts and figures, but when the great day came he was floored by his guest's very first question. Sweeping his hand over the entire campus, he asked, 'Now tell me, what is all this for?' The teacher's head was so crammed with dates and statistics that for a few moments the question left him speechless and all his careful preparation seemed irrelevant.

Of course he soon recovered his poise and was able to give a clear account of the school's overall purpose, but the story has a global parallel. With millions of pounds being poured into making the arrival of the year 2000 the greatest event since Ethelred the Unready was King of the English, most people are ignoring the one fundamental question that demands to be answered: *what is it all about*? Why should the year 2000 attract any more attention than 1569, 1823 or 1981? Is it nothing more than the appeal of a nice, even number? Does it have any historical, political, religious or other significance? Is there any reason why we should treat it differently from any other year? Why all the fuss? To repeat the fundamental question: what is it all about?

There *is* an answer. This book will tell you what it is.

1.
Y2K

In countries all around the world, national commissions are planning a bewildering variety of activities to welcome in the new millennium. The outlay of time, energy — and cash — is phenomenal. No expense is being spared to make this the biggest party our planet has ever known, and day after day the media are churning out facts and figures about events being planned and ideas being pursued.

- In the United States, New York aims to have the biggest and best party of all, starting at the moment the millennium dawns over the South Pacific.
- In Britain, over £1.2 billion is being spent on London's Millennium Dome, which is hoping to bring the New Millennium Experience to millions of visitors during the year.
- In Australia, Sydney plans to stage the most spectacular fireworks party the world has ever seen.
- Ireland has already jumped the gun, and in March 1999 linked its annual St Patrick's Day celebrations with the

new millennium in putting on the largest fireworks display ever seen in the Northern Hemisphere.
• One of New Zealand's projects is a huge Millennium TimeVault. A treasury of ethnic, cultural, religious and sporting icons will be sealed in a massive pyramid-shaped container, which is to remain unopened until the year 3000.
• In Italy, Rome is expecting at least thirty million visitors to celebrate the millennium in the 'Eternal City'.

Needless to say, those with an eye to the main chance are aiming to cash in. Edinburgh's Balmoral Hotel is charging £8,500 per couple for a special three-day millennium package, yet even this must seem pretty down-market to the Sultan of Brunei, who has offered £67,000 a night (he may be outbid) for the Villa La Cupola Suite at Rome's Hotel Excelsior.

Eating out will not be cheap on 31 December 1999. A five-course dinner at London's Lanesborough Hotel will set you back £2,000. This does include indoor fireworks and a singer, but still seems extortionate when one of my local Italian restaurants offers a perfectly acceptable meal for a mere £400 a head!

As to the best place to be when midnight strikes, Greenwich, Fiji, the Cook Islands and Australia's Great Barrier Reef are among the front runners. The Bristol-based company Wild Wings offers a flight in a Mig 25 Foxbat Fighter aircraft, which can reach a height of 80,000 feet, enabling passengers to see in the millennium from the edge of space. The Scottish organization Millennium 2000 is planning a trip which takes in both Fiji and the Cook Islands, so that its clients can greet the new millennium twice. Not to be outdone, another company is offering east-to-west flights on the supersonic Concorde, enabling passengers to get three new millennia for the price of one. Some of those with a taste for the quirky are already booked on Orient Lines' sixteen-day Millennium Antarctic cruise. As the sun never sets in Antarctica, they will see in the year 2000 without ever literally witnessing the dawn of the new millennium.

Of course the celebration is not to be confined to one day, nor will it be limited to eating, drinking, partying and holiday-making. In Britain alone, hundreds of major projects are being planned to coincide with the new millennium. In London, two new bridges are to be built across the River Thames. Belfast is to have six new community parks. Cardiff will get a 75,000-seater Millennium Stadium. Glasgow is building two new Children's Centres. Newcastle is working on a science-based, high-tech International Centre for Life. Liverpool is looking forward to a multi-media Discovery Centre. Determined not to be left behind, the Isle of Wight is building a Dinosaur Museum and Botanical Gardens.

The bug

Yet for all the mounting excitement about the forthcoming festivities, one dark cloud looms on the horizon — the so-called millennium bug. The bug was born in the early days of computers. In order to save space, programmers used only two digits for each year (i.e. '73' for '1973') and computers 'assumed' that the two missing digits were '19'. This will work perfectly well until 31 December 1999, but on the following day, when the year shows up as '00', computers not built or adjusted to act differently will decode this as '1900', freeze up, or generate false data. With our modern dependence on computerized technology, the theoretical potential for catastrophe is almost endless, and some 750,000 websites are dedicated to the problem. Here are some of the dire predictions that have been made:

• Multiple sections of national electricity grids could shut down (in mid-winter for one half of the world), with horrific consequences. One North American writer foresees thousands of people dying from cold, hunger, crime and disease and at least 70% of Americans losing their jobs or their present level of income by April 2000.

• Supplies of drinking water dependent on electricity to run the pumps that deliver it could dry up. My own local water company recently wrote telling me that it was spending £15 million to deal with 'predictable problems', while cautiously adding, 'No one can give an absolute guarantee on every aspect of this problem.'

• Hospital equipment, including machines used for diagnosis, treatment, monitoring and life support, could shut down, resulting in severe medical complications and widespread deaths.

• Worldwide banking could collapse. According to a *Sunday Times* article, 'This is not a prediction, it is a certainty — there will be a serious disruption of the world's financial services industry.' A highly-placed economic forecaster has predicted 'a severe global recession'. Others are encouraging investors to withdraw substantial sums of money just prior to the end of December — advice leading to the suggestion that banks will not be able to cope with the demand. The United States Federal Reserve Board has said it will set aside an extra $50 billion of currency reserves to help in any emergency.

• Nuclear missiles could be launched accidentally. American and Russian scientists have been working on a 'shared early warning centre' to prevent this.

• Businesses of every kind could be badly hit, with communications shut down for days or even weeks on end. With just months to go, the British government was still running press advertisements warning that 75% of organizations which thought they were ready for the new millennium were not. Companies were urged to get in touch with Action 2000, set up by the government to help in checking machinery, office equipment and security systems. One software expert has called the millennium bug 'the biggest business problem in human history'.

• Airline schedules may suffer severe disruption, cancellations — or worse — and some have already decided that none of their planes will be airborne at midnight on 31 December 1999.

Up to £60 billion is being invested worldwide in countering the millennium bug, but many of those who feel that even this is 'too little, too late' are taking no chances.

In the United States, hundreds of cities have formed community preparation groups, urging local officials to set up emergency food banks, shelters and power generators. Some people have already sold their urban homes and moved to rural areas, where they are building underground living quarters powered by wind and solar panels and stock-piling tinned and dehydrated foods, drugs and medicines. One of them told a reporter, 'If I'm right, I'm going to look pretty smart. And if I'm wrong, I'll have a lifetime supply of canned tuna.' For people who are unsure what to do, one source offers *The Millennial Bug Personal Survival Kit* and another a six-part audio-tape series and 'preparedness manual' entitled *Countdown to Chaos*.

TEOTWAWKI?

Updated reports of progress in killing off the millennium bug paint a more hopeful picture and suggest that, while there may be problems, panic is out of place. Yet even if we could be assured that the bothersome bug will be safely dead and buried by December 1999, this would not put an end to predictions of TEOTWAWKI — The End Of The World As We Know It.

The turn of every century has produced a rash of predictions that our world was about to end in one way or another, and the approach of a new millennium is turning the rash into an epidemic. As the year 1000 approached, it was widely believed that this might bring down the curtain. The year 1260 was in the frame for a while. A Roman Catholic priest wrote a book predicting the end of the world in 1847; the church gave him permission to publish it in 1848. The heretical Jehovah's Witnesses cult has backed a whole string of losers — 1874, 1914, 1915 and 1975. In the 1970s, the American author Hal Lindsey wrote a runaway best-seller entitled *The Late Great Planet Earth*, forecasting the end of the present world order within one generation of the founding of the modern state of Israel in 1948. In 1988, another American, Edgar Whisenant, hit the charts with a book listing eighty-eight reasons why he believed this would happen between 11-13 September of that year.

In spite of these and numerous other failures, TEOTWAWKI prophecies are still flourishing. Astronomers predict an alignment of planets in May 2000 which some scientists believe could disrupt the tilt of the earth's axis, or dislodge one or both polar ice caps. This would lead to massive killer earthquakes and an invasion of lethal microbes which present medical resources would not be able to counter. One group of astrologers says that Chiron and Pluto will form a conjunction on 31 December 1999 and that this represents 'the most appropriate astrological symbol for leaving the past behind'. An increasing number of destructive religious cults anticipate the end of the world within the next year or two. These and other prophets of doom are beginning to eat into the public psyche: a recent survey showed about 20% of Americans believing that the world will come to an end in or around the year 2000.

Cult activity linked to the millennium is causing concern in law-enforcement agencies. Scotland Yard and the
FBI are mounting a major security operation to guard
against cults staging mass suicides or terrorist attacks. In
London, a water-borne unit will provide a twenty-four
hour patrol at the site of the Millennium Dome. In
America, the FBI is concentrating surveillance on the
group of north-western states sometimes known as
'kooks' corner'. In Israel, security forces are taking steps
to counter the so-called 'Jerusalem syndrome' thought
to exist among certain groups of religious extremists.
Some suspected trouble-makers have already been de-
ported, but fears remain that the dawn of a new millennium will provide the chance of a lifetime for spectacular
mass martyrdom.

Etcetera...

Groups with less violent ideas are framing more optimis-
tic agendas. The Lightshift Global Meditation Initiative
says that, as a change of day, month, year, decade, century and millennium will all happen at once, 'The energy
of a thousand New Year's Eves will be amplified in the
hearts and minds of all the peoples on planet Earth.' It
urges millions of us to band together 'in the quantum
numbers necessary to create a powerful circuit of light to
greet the dawn of the new millennium', in order to produce 'the most powerful and positive shift in human history'. According to LGMI, even one-tenth of one per

cent of the world's population uniting in this way could 'create the pilot light to ignite the divinity in all humanity'. This may be unadulterated psychobabble, but millions are falling for it.

Others weave a selection of beguiling phrases together to give meaning to their millennial plans. In the United States, the White House will lead 'a wide variety of activities and initiatives designed to highlight our heritage and celebrate our creativity'. Some speak of 'celebrating the triumph of the human spirit', of 'celebrating achievements in science and the arts', of 'marking a thousand years of invention and discovery' and of 'producing a greater sense of understanding and appreciation of people from different backgrounds'. In Britain, an ecumenical organization is hoping to unite the nation in a Millennium Moment and in reciting this official Millennium Resolution: 'Let there be respect for the earth, peace for its people, love in our lives, delight in the good, forgiveness for past wrongs, and from now on a new start.' In spite of its obvious weaknesses (no central focus, no common theme, no historical context and no mention of a deity who might enable us to achieve these admirable aims) millions will doubtless join in, using the Millennium Candle to be provided for every family in the country.

One way or another, the year 2000, sometimes called Y2000 and even more crisply known as Y2K, looks unlikely to arrive quietly.

2.
A birth and a book

What happened exactly twenty centuries before 1 January 2000 that has produced such a phenomenal focus on Y2K? The answer is very simple and, in view of all the excitement, may seem quite strange. *Nothing happened* — nothing, at least, which gives us the slightest reason for getting excited about the big day ahead. On 'day zero', the sun rose and set, rivers flowed, birds flew, fish swam and animals did what animals do. Babies were born, some people had accidents, a number fell in love, others got married and many died, but history records nothing which can begin to explain why Y2K is getting the world into such a lather.

Day zero

We know this for the simple reason that we can no longer trace 'day zero'. Primitive man measured his calendar by the movement of the sun and the phases of the moon, though the system now used in the Western world is linked to the ancient Hebrew calendar. It was based on what its founders believed to be the date of the creation of the world, and had a thirteenth month inserted every nineteen years. This calendar did not come into general use until the ninth century, when a critical dating mistake of five years was made, and there have been several other major complications since. By the time Julius Caesar (c.100-44 B.C.) came to power, dates had become muddled by politics, leading him to make certain adjustments. These lasted until the sixteenth century, but by this time the calendar year was thirteen days behind the solar year. To correct this, Pope Gregory XIII (1502-1585) directed that ten days in 1582 should be dropped, the day after 4 October becoming 15 October. The so-called Gregorian calendar was not universally accepted at the time, and was not adopted in Britain until 1752, when 3-13 September were dropped (protesters took to the streets shouting, 'Give us back our eleven days!') and New Year's Day was moved from 25 March to 1 January.

All of this juggling makes it easy to see why we have problems locating 'day zero'. Nor are things helped by our being told that the Royal Greenwich Observatory, the US Naval Observatory, the Encyclopaedia Britannica and the World Almanac all agree that, because of another hitch in the year 526, the third millennium does not officially begin until 1 January 2001 and that all the hoo-ha is happening twelve months early! Be that as it may, a major clue in discovering the meaning of what we have chosen to celebrate as the millennial year is that it is called 'A.D. 2000'. 'A.D.' is an abbreviation for the Latin phrase *Anno*

Domini, which means 'in the year of the Lord'. This tells us that our calendar is keyed, not to some gigantic natural event, such as a falling meteorite, an earthquake or a catastrophic flood, but to a human being who was given the title 'Lord'. Whether or not the title is appropriate is irrelevant at this point, but there has only ever been one person linked to its use in connection with our present dating system — a man born approximately 2,000 years ago.

At first glance, he seems a strange choice. He was born into a blue-collar family living in a nondescript town (Nazareth) in a remote part (Galilee) of one of the world's smallest countries (Palestine). For about thirty years, almost nothing he said or did seems to have attracted any attention outside his own family circle. About three years later he was dead yet, as we enter the twenty-first century, millions of people would agree with the verdict of the British novelist H. G. Wells who said that nobody could write a history of the human race without giving him the 'first and foremost place'. Wells' Russian counterpart Fyodor Dostoevsky said much the same thing: 'Not only is there no one else like him, but there could never be anyone like him.' If these assessments seem 'over the top', think about the following facts:

- We have no record of his date of birth ('day zero'), yet the whole of history, in the Western world at least, is now divided into the years before he was born and those which followed his birth, even though we are about five years adrift in our calculations.

- He never wrote a book, yet more books have been written about him than about any other person. The nearest thing we have to his biography has now been translated in whole or in part into well over 2,000 languages, and in a recent five-year period more books about him were published than in the previous fifty years.
- He never painted a picture, composed any poetry, or wrote any music, yet nobody's life and teaching have inspired a greater number of songs, plays, poetry, films, videos and other art forms. One film based almost entirely on his recorded words has been produced in more than 500 languages and has already been seen by more people than any other film in history.
- He never raised an army or led an armed rebellion, yet millions of people have laid down their lives in his cause, and thousands still do so every year.
- Except for one brief period during his childhood, his travels were limited to an area about the size of Wales, but his influence today is worldwide and his followers constitute the largest religious grouping the world has ever known.
- He had no formal education, but thousands of universities, seminaries, colleges and schools have been founded in his name.
- His public life lasted just three years, and was restricted to a few parts of one small country, yet purpose-built satellites and some of the world's largest radio and television networks now beam his teaching around the world.
- He set foot in just two countries, yet an organization committed to his cause claims to make regular flights to

more countries than any of the world's commercial airlines.

- During his lifetime, he was virtually unknown outside of his own nation, yet in the current issue of *Encyclopaedia Britannica* the entry under his name runs to 30,000 words.

Do Wells and Dostoevsky still sound 'over the top'? Nobody in history has attracted more attention than the man whose birth triggered off Y2K. For twenty centuries, every recorded word he spoke has been meticulously analysed by theologians, philosophers and others. On the day I am writing these words (and on the day you are reading them) several million people are studying what he said and did and trying to apply the significance of his words and actions to their own lives. Can any serious-minded person ignore someone with these credentials? Who exactly was he? What makes him so special? Why is he still such a dynamic force when the rich and famous of his era are now nothing more than footnotes on the pages of history? The answers may surprise you. *They may do much more.*

Database

His name was Jesus, sometimes known as Jesus of Nazareth to distinguish him from the many contemporaries with the same name. The atheistic British philosopher Bertrand Russell once wrote, 'Historically, it is quite doubtful whether Jesus ever existed at all, and if he did we do not know anything about him,' but this is prejudiced non-sense. A number of distinguished first-century authors (who shared Russell's atheism, but were somewhat better placed to assess the facts) record more than 100 details about Jesus' birth, life and death, all without the slightest hint that he was not a real, historical person, and the British historian James Frazar is right to say that any doubts cast on whether Jesus ever existed are 'unworthy of serious attention'.

Most of the first-hand information we have about Jesus is found in the Bible. That being the case, we need to make an important detour before we go any further. Just as Jesus is the most remarkable person in history, so the Bible is its most remarkable book. Although it has been the target of twenty centuries of vicious opposition and relentless scepticism, its integrity remains unscathed and its influence unequalled. Anyone who tries to rubbish the Bible, or even to reduce it to the level of a 'good book', has to overcome the following facts:

- We have more manuscripts of biblical material than we have of any other ancient document (over 25,000, as against 643 of the runner-up, Homer's *Iliad*).
- The copies we have are vastly superior to those of any ancient document. In the judgement of Sir Frederic Kenyon, one-time director and principal librarian of the British Museum, 'It cannot be too strongly asserted that in substance the text of the Bible is certain... *This can be said of no other ancient book in the world.*'

• Although documents from that period are notoriously unreliable, the Bible's history is amazingly accurate. After forty-five years of concentrated study of the subject, the outstanding American scholar Robert Dick Wilson, one-time Professor of Semitic Philology (the language and literature of the Middle East) at Princeton University, concluded that, over a period of nearly 4,000 years, Old Testament data had been transmitted 'with the most minute accuracy'. In assessing the Bible's recorded details of forty kings living over a period of 1,600 years he said, 'Mathematically, it is one chance in 750,000,000,000,000,000,000,000,000 that this accuracy is mere circumstance.'

• Archaeology is constantly unearthing material confirming the Bible's detailed data. The evidence of archaeology is so powerful that Nelson Glueck, often considered the dean of Palestinian archaeology, has written of 'the almost incredibly accurate historical memory of the Bible' and has gone so far as to say, 'It may be stated categorically that *no archaeological discovery has ever controverted a biblical reference.*'

• The Bible speaks with a uniquely united voice. It is not so much a book as a library of sixty-six documents, written by some forty different authors at intervals stretching over more than 1,500 years. These men lived at different times, in a variety of cultures and came from different levels of society. If asked about any controversial subject, they would have had views as diverse as those heard on any of today's media chat shows. Yet, without any collaboration or spin-doctoring, they combined to produce a single volume which is amazingly coherent.

After many years of studying its contents, the modern British scholar J. I. Packer says that the Bible holds together in a way that is 'simply stunning' and adds, 'The inner unity of the Bible is miraculous: a sign and wonder challenging the unbelief of our sceptical age.'

• There are many places in which the Bible stakes its own integrity on the truth of its prophecies. Unlike claims by today's astrologers, soothsayers, crystal-ball gazers, compilers of horoscopes, readers of palms and tea leaves, and other assorted con artists, *not even one of the Bible's prophecies can be shown to be false*. What are the odds against this? Peter Stoner, a charter member of the American Scientific Affiliation, has calculated the probability of just seven of these prophecies being fulfilled by chance, and has put it at one in 5,000,000,000. Sceptics sometimes say that statistics can be made to prove anything, but this one is pretty impressive — and the Bible has not just seven prophecies but several hundred!

These facts alone should be sufficient to get the attention of anyone who is prepared to assess the Bible with an open mind, but two other factors can be added. The first is that in spite of twenty centuries of more or less relentless attack (including, in recent times, Marxism's determined efforts to destroy it) the Bible remains the world's best-selling book, with hundreds of millions of copies being published every year in some 2,200 languages.

The second is the massive influence the Bible has had, not merely in the lives of individuals but on the moral climate of communities and nations. Commenting on social progress in the country around the beginning of the seventeenth century, historian John Richard Green wrote, 'No greater moral change ever passed over a nation than passed over England... England became the people of a book, and that book was the Bible.' Many of the profound social changes which took place in Britain during the nineteenth century were spearheaded by people who took their lead from the Bible. William Wilberforce was the driving force behind the abolition of slavery. Elizabeth Fry revolutionized the treatment of women in prisons. Lord Shaftesbury did the same for working conditions among the poorer classes and campaigned against the opium drug trade, child prostitution and cruelty to animals. Thomas Barnardo established homes which, during his own lifetime, provided a refuge for 60,000 destitute children. These and others like them gave the clearest possible testimony that the Bible was the source of their principles and the secret of their power.

These people hit the headlines, but the small print is even more impressive. All around the world today, millions of people claim that the Bible is changing their lives for the better, giving them a coherent world-view, a set of consistent ethical principles, a sense of purpose and a moral dynamic they had never known before. Charles Colson, special counsel to United States President Richard Nixon in the early 1970s, served time in prison because of his part in the notorious Watergate affair which led to Nixon's downfall. Later, Colson's life was transformed by the Bible's teaching and he added this assessment of its influence to his own personal testimony:

'Nothing has affected the rise and fall of civilization, the character of cultures, the structure of government, and the lives of the inhabitants of this planet as profoundly as the words of the Bible.'

The Bible's teaching has sometimes been twisted out of shape and used to justify the kind of behaviour it condemns outright, but the fact remains that after nearly 2,000 years its accuracy, integrity, unity, prophecy and authority remain unequalled. Why should this be so? Why has nothing else come even close to matching it? The Bible itself answers the question and its open secret is that its words came into being when 'men spoke from God as they were carried along by the Holy Spirit'.[1] If the Bible is trustworthy (and all the evidence we can lay our hands on says it is) then *we must take seriously its claim that it is more than trustworthy*. When we do, we find that, far from being a merely human compilation of history and ideas, it is the 'living and enduring word of God'.[2] The rest of this book is written on that basis.

3.
Fantasy and the facts

There has never been a shortage of opinions about Jesus, either during his lifetime or in the nearly 2,000 years since. Ignoring the Bible's own teaching (we will come to that later) and all the garbled or watered-down versions of it that have been offered, there has been an almost endless list of ideas about him, ranging from the blasphemous to the bizarre.

Soon after he had burst on the public scene, 'There was widespread whispering about him. Some said, "He is a good man." Others replied, "No, he deceives the people." '[3] A little later, 'The people were divided.'[4] At one point, local religious leaders said, 'This man is not from God', while others were more straightforward and dismissed him as 'a sinner'.[5] While he was in Caesarea Philippi, a snapshot poll showed some people thinking he was the recently murdered preacher John the Baptist come back to life, and others that he was a reincarnation of Elijah, Jeremiah, or one of the other Old Testament prophets, all of whom had died over 400 years earlier.[6]

At one time or another he was accused of being in league with the devil,[7] alleged to be 'demon-possessed and raving mad',[8] branded as 'a glutton and a drunkard',[9] and charged with being a blasphemer[10] and a law-breaker.[11] On more than one occasion he was heavily criticized for mixing too freely with the local riff-raff[12] and he was eventually accused of treason against the country's Roman government.[13]

Twenty centuries later, Jesus remains the focus of highly controversial attention. In 1984, London Weekend Television screened a three-part programme called *Jesus — The Evidence*, in which they had invested two years and nearly £400,000, and came up with a rag-bag of theories, including those which saw Jesus as a hypnotist, an occultist, a magician and a sexual deviant. Founded in the United States in 1995, the so-called Jesus Seminar said that the Bible's picture was grossly distorted and declared its own intention 'to rescue Jesus from the spin doctors' and replace him with a 'new and improved Jesus' who would fit more easily into today's world. In the film *The Last Temptation of Christ*, released a few years ago, Jesus is portrayed as a rampant New Ager (calling stones and earth 'my body') and confesses to being a liar and a hypocrite, while the film's main focus has him riddled with sexual hang-ups.

Others take an even more radical line, and go beyond criticism of his integrity and morality to questioning his identity. In 1970, the philologist John Allegro suggested that, far from being a historical figure, Jesus was no more than the code-word for an ancient sex-cult inspired by a hallucinogenic mushroom. This did nothing to enhance Allegro's academic reputation and, in the words of one critic, 'gave mushrooms a bad name'!

The rumour factory is still in production. Jesus has been called a political revolutionary, a religious guru, a mystic channeller, an impersonal life force and some kind of faith healer. In their book *The Holy Blood and the Holy Grail*, M. Baigent, R. Leigh and H. Lincoln claim that Jesus was an intergalactic freedom fighter who came to earth and married, and that his descendants are secretly plotting to take over Europe.

What are we to make of all this? In 1994, a *Life* magazine article said, 'We see Jesus in our own image,' implying that people tend to make up a picture of Jesus that fits in with their own psychological needs. The article saw nothing wrong with this, and suggested that a kaleidoscope of ideas helps us to get a better understanding of Jesus, but this is absurd, as many of the pictures contradict virtually all the others. Robert Funk, founder of the Jesus Seminar, claimed that 'What we need is a new fiction,' but what we really need is to get back to the old facts. Why settle for man's speculation when we have access to God's revelation?

One of us

Some of the theories I have mentioned are so hare-brained that before going any further we need to establish that, although Jesus stands out from the rest of humankind, he does so as a genuine human being, not as some kind of biological freak, genetic hybrid or extra-terrestrial alien. The Bible traces his family back through forty generations without the slightest hint of any abnormality, and the New Testament provides us with four clear pieces of evidence to show that he was fully, truly and totally human.

1. *His physical life*

As we shall see in the next chapter, he had a perfectly normal birth. After pregnancy, his mother Mary 'gave birth to her firstborn, a son'.[14] Like any other Jewish boy, he was circumcised when he was eight days old.[15] (Circumcision was an important Jewish practice, laid down in the Old Testament as a sign of God's covenant with his chosen people.) He experienced all the normal phases of physical development. In one chapter alone, he is described as a 'baby',[16] a 'child'[17] and a 'boy'.[18] He had to be taught to crawl, stand, walk, feed himself, wash, dress, write and go to the toilet. His hair grew, his muscles expanded, his voice broke, he passed through puberty into manhood. He also showed that he had all the usual physical limitations. He needed food[19] and drink.[20] After a hard day's travelling he was 'tired ... from the journey'.[21] He needed sleep.[22] He knew what it was to be physically weakened by suffering and stress.[23] Soon after he died, his body was pierced with a spear, and medical experts say that an eyewitness's report of a 'sudden flow of blood and water'[24] is exactly how a layman might describe blood and serum pouring from a post-mortem rupture of the pericardial sac.

2. His intellectual life

Just as he had normal physical limitations (he could not stand on the day he was born, jump 100 feet in the air, or be in two places at once), so he had intellectual limitations. While there is no record of his getting any facts wrong, he 'grew in wisdom'[25] and from time to time there were apparently things he did not know. When faced with a crowd of hungry people, he asked his followers, 'How many loaves do you have?'[26] When a distraught father brought his demon-possessed son to him, he asked, 'How long has he been like this?'[27] When he visited Bethany four days after a friend had died, he enquired, 'Where have you laid him?'[28]

3. His emotional life

Like any other human being, Jesus experienced a great range of emotions. He called his immediate followers 'friends'.[29] Of a particularly close relationship with one family, we are told that 'Jesus loved Martha and her sister and Lazarus.'[30] There were times when he showed flashes of anger. When people tried to stop parents bringing their children to him, he was 'indignant'.[31] Nor was he a great fan of political correctness: he called the crafty King Herod 'that fox',[32] false prophets 'ferocious wolves'[33] and Pharisees a 'brood of vipers',[34] 'blind fools',[35] 'whitewashed tombs'[36] and 'hypocrites'.[37] When he saw blackmarketeering and swindling going on in the temple in Jerusalem, he drove the racketeers out in an explosion of anger.[38] At other times, he showed great sorrow: looking over Jerusalem at a time when it was on the brink of disaster, 'he wept over it'.[39] He showed great sympathy and compassion: when he came across a deaf mute, he expressed his feelings with 'a deep sigh',[40] and when he saw crowds of people in religious and spiritual confusion, he 'had compassion on them'.[41] Parts of his teaching had humorous undertones, and on receiving good news from his friends, he was 'full of joy'.[42]

4. His spiritual life

He knew all about the struggle against the forces of evil and the pressure to conform to the degenerate moral climate of his day. We are specifically told that he was 'tempted in every way, just as we are'.[43] He prayed: there are twenty-five specific instances on record, and we can be sure that these represented a lifetime of prayer. He regularly attended public worship: 'On the Sabbath day he went into the synagogue, as was his custom.'[44] He also studied the Bible: he was constantly quoting the Old Testament and, with one exception, he did so from memory.

In these four areas we have all the evidence we need to show that Jesus was not an alien, a monster, a biological freak, or some kind of ghost in a skin. He was everything that we mean when we speak of a human being. He was one of us.

4.
Close encounters

A few weeks ago, one of my daughters-in-law went to
the doctor to hear the result of a test. The look on his
face gave the game away before he told her the result: 'It
is positive: you are pregnant.' Debbie and her husband
Stephen were delighted, as are millions of married couples
every year when they hear similar news. Yet to hard-
pressed parents, pregnancy sometimes comes tinged with
disappointment, while it can be a sickening jolt to unmar-
ried teenagers who have to face up to consequences they
had hoped to avoid.

   In the case of Jesus' mother, her reaction was one of
utter amazement, not because she had always practised
'safe sex', but for a much more radical reason: she was a
virgin. When speaking about the Bible's account of the
beginning of Jesus' earthly life, people often refer to the
'Virgin Birth', but this phrase can be misleading, as there
is no evidence of anything unusual about his birth. As far
as we know, he left his mother's womb by the usual biological processes. The startling thing is not how he *left*
his mother's womb, but how he *entered* it, and in this the

Bible could not be more emphatic. It says that Jesus was conceived in his mother's womb without sexual intercourse and without the injection of male sperm in any other way. In medical terms, his mother became pregnant while she was *virgo intacta*. As if that were not remarkable enough, she was given the news, not by her GP, but by an angel.

Who believes in miracles?

For many people, the last two sentences are enough to discredit the whole story. A woman becoming pregnant without receiving any male sperm, and the diagnosis being announced by an angel? This means miracles, and as miracles are on a par with fairy tales we can safely write the whole thing off — or can we?

What is a miracle? A working definition would be an event or action which apparently contradicts known scientific laws, and for some people that is precisely what rules it out. Anything which contradicts the scientific laws operating within our closed-world system of time and space can be rejected. This argument used to sound like an open-and-shut case, but it is pretty much out of date by now, especially since Einstein's theory of relativity changed our understanding of the universe. The eminent British lawyer Professor Sir Norman Anderson says that 'Physicists, doctors and others have come increasingly to realize that the exceptional and the unexpected does happen from time to time and that cause and effect do not invariably follow the normal pattern.' Rejecting the possibility of miracles on scientific grounds is decidedly unscientific!

In 1994, the theologically liberal Bishop of Durham hit the headlines by casting doubt on the virgin conception of Jesus (bishops, after all, are meant to support the Bible's teaching, not sabotage it). Among those who rejected the bishop's scepticism were fourteen eminent scientists, most of them university professors. In a letter to *The Times* they wrote, 'It is not logically valid to use science as an argument against miracles. *To believe that miracles cannot happen is as much an act of faith as to believe that they can happen...* Miracles are unprecedented events. Whatever the current fashions in philosophy or the revelations of opinion polls may suggest, it is important to affirm that science (based as it is on the observation of precedents) *can have nothing to say on the subject.*' As long ago as the seventeenth century, the French genius Blaise Pascal (philosopher, physicist, mathematician and theologian) said, 'It is impossible on reasonable grounds to destroy miracles.'

What about the 'current fashions in philosophy' mentioned in the letter to *The Times*? These often make the same mistake by denying that miracles can happen before they examine the evidence. As the brilliant British author C. S. Lewis wrote, 'Those who assume that miracles cannot happen are merely wasting their time by looking into the texts: we know in advance what results they will find, for they have begun by begging the question.' The Scottish author, broadcaster (and atheist) Sir Ludovic Kennedy provides a recent example of this. In his book *All In The*

Mind, published in 1999, he assures us that 'Miracles don't happen' but as his book is subtitled 'A Farewell to God' we know what he thinks about miracles before we read the first page. The fact that he produces no evidence to back up his argument hardly helps his case.

For most people, the problem about accepting miracles lies not in the quality of the evidence but in the presuppositions which they bring to the issue. Yet unless we deny the existence of God, what grounds do we have for rejecting the possibility that he may at times choose to work in unusual ways which contrast with his ordinary way of working. Is anybody qualified to do this?

As soon as we bring God into the reckoning, the whole picture changes. Since God framed the laws which govern the universe, surely he has the right to bring other laws into play whenever he chooses? Once we accept God's independent, supernatural power and authority, we have no scientific, philosophical or logical reason for disbelieving any of his actions. God is not stuck in a rut, unable to do anything new or different. However spectacular they may seem to us, miracles are hardly a problem to the one who is Sovereign of a universe which he brought into being as easily as we clap our hands. In God's mind, there is no distinction between 'natural' and 'supernatural', because what we call the supernatural is God's lifestyle. God never sees miracles as emergency measures; instead, everything he does is consistent with his own wise, loving and eternal purposes.

It is interesting to note that neither of the Bible's basic languages (Hebrew and Greek) has a word which exactly corresponds to our understanding of 'miracle'. Instead, there are words which we can properly translate 'wonders'[45] (things which excite attention and awe), or 'signs'[46] (which, because they are so extraordinary, refer to action by God). The English word 'miracle' is one which we have invented to cover these concepts. Ultimately, the question is not '*Can* miracles happen?' but '*Have* they happened?', and each case must be examined in the light of the evidence. Then what about the case in hand, the virgin conception of Jesus?

Case notes

Quite apart from the overriding fact that the Bible is the Word of God, it is interesting to notice that the two main narratives of the conception and birth of Jesus were written by two men whose occupations called for accuracy of expression and attention to detail: Matthew was a civil servant and Luke a doctor. This is Luke's account:

> In the sixth month, God sent the angel Gabriel to Nazareth, a town in Galilee, to a virgin pledged to be married to a man named Joseph, a descendant of David. The virgin's name was Mary. The angel went to her and said, 'Greetings, you who are highly favoured! The Lord is with you.'
> Mary was greatly troubled at his words and wondered what kind of greeting this might be. But the angel said to her, 'Do not be afraid, Mary, you have found favour with God. You will be with child

and give birth to a son, and you are to give him the name Jesus. He will be great and will be called the Son of the Most High. The Lord God will give him the throne of his father David, and he will reign over the house of Jacob for ever; his kingdom will never end.'

'How will this be,' Mary asked the angel, 'since I am a virgin?'

The angel answered: 'The Holy Spirit will come upon you, and the power of the Most High will overshadow you. So the holy one to be born will be called the Son of God. Even Elizabeth your relative is going to have a child in her old age, and she who was said to be barren is in her sixth month. For nothing is impossible with God.'

'I am the Lord's servant,' Mary answered. 'May it be to me as you have said.' Then the angel left her.[47]

It is easy to understand why Mary was 'greatly troubled'. Seeing an angel was hardly an everyday occurrence, and being told (in pre-scanning times) that the embryo would be male was bewildering enough, let alone receiving instructions from God as to what her son was to be called. Yet there was something even more puzzling. How could all this come about when she was a virgin? Whatever the angel might say, how could one argue with the facts of life? The angel's response was to say that God would work a biological miracle in her womb, bringing about a virgin conception which would lead to the birth of a baby boy who would not be the son of her husband Joseph but in a unique way the Son of God.

To assure her that God was perfectly capable of over-riding the natural order of things, the angel reminded her that an elderly relative, Elizabeth, well past child-bearing age, was already six months pregnant. As Mary knew this, she quietly accepted that, for reasons beyond her understanding, she had been chosen to fulfil a unique role in human history.

The husband's part

The doctor's report is concise and clear, and it is worth noticing that Mary's virginity is mentioned not once but three times. Matthew's account involves Joseph:

> This is how the birth of Jesus Christ came about: His mother Mary was pledged to be married to Joseph, but before they came together, she was found to be with child through the Holy Spirit. Because Joseph her husband was a righteous man and did not want to expose her to public disgrace, he had in mind to divorce her quietly.
>
> But after he had considered this, an angel of the Lord appeared to him in a dream and said, 'Joseph, son of David, do not be afraid to take Mary home as your wife, because what is conceived in her is from the Holy Spirit. She will give birth to a son, and you are to give him the name Jesus, because he will save his people from their sins.'[48]

A little later Matthew ends his narrative like this:

> When Joseph woke up, he did what the angel of
> the Lord had commanded him and took Mary home
> as his wife. But he had no union with her until she
> gave birth to a son. And he gave him the name
> Jesus.[49]

There were three stages in traditional Jewish marriage
procedure. The first was an *engagement* (more of an ar-
rangement than an engagement as we know it today),
which sometimes took place when the two people concerned were still children. The second was the *betrothal*,
when the man and woman pledged themselves to each
other in the presence of witnesses. Though continuing to
live separately, they would be called 'husband' and 'wife'
(Matthew uses these very words) and the step was so
serious that it could be undone only by divorce. This state
of being pledged lasted for about a year, after which the
couple came together in *marriage*.

As Matthew makes clear, it was during the 'betrothal'
stage that Mary found herself pregnant. As Joseph knew
he was not the father, he could only assume that Mary
had been sleeping with someone else. Rather than go
through a very public divorce before a magistrate, when
Mary would be forced to confess her immorality in open
court, he decided on a second option available to him.
This was to divorce her 'quietly', when papers could be
signed privately in the presence of just two witnesses.
While Joseph was getting ready to do this, an angel inter-
vened and encouraged him to go through with the

marriage because Mary's pregnancy was the result of a
unique act of God. Matthew then tells us that the marriage went ahead as planned, but he underlines the significant fact that Joseph 'had no union with her until she
gave birth to a son'. As we are told later in the New Testament that Jesus had brothers and sisters,[50] it is clear that
Joseph and Mary had normal sexual relations after Jesus
was born, but Matthew joins Luke in confirming that prior
to his birth Mary remained a virgin.

The doubters

Over the centuries, there have always been sceptics will-
ing to look for any explanation rather than accept what
the Bible says. One line of approach has been to say that
the New Testament narratives were invented to match or
outdo tales of how certain pagan gods and religious leaders came into being. There are some exciting examples
on offer. Buddha's mother claimed that her son was born
ten months after a white elephant with six tusks 'entered
my belly'. Hinduism claims that the divine Vishnu, after
several reincarnations as a fish, a tortoise, a bear and a
lion, descended into the womb of Devali and was born as
her son, the hero Krishna. The mother of the Greek god
Perseus was said to have been impregnated by a shower
of rain containing Zeus, the king of the gods. Zeus seems
to have been decidedly promiscuous (and a master of dis-
guise) as he is also said to have fathered Alexander the
Great as the result of taking the form of a serpent and
seducing Olympus, the wife of Philip of Macedon. This is

rousing stuff, but the idea that Jesus' conception is another such yarn is hopelessly flawed. There is no evidence that the New Testament writers had even heard of these exotic fantasies, and their crude sensuality is in stark contrast to the simplicity and purity of the Bible's narrative.

One compromise solution has been to say that, although it would make it unique in human culture, the virgin conception was a case of parthenogenesis (the female egg dividing itself without male fertilization). However, this theory collapses because of the genetic make-up of human beings. While the male has x and y chromosomes, the female has x and x. This means that if Mary's pregnancy had been triggered off by some biological freak the child born as a result would have been female, as no y chromosome would have been present to produce a male. Those who use this argument to deny the virgin conception replace the report of a miraculous fact with the rumour of a miraculous fantasy!

Questions

The virgin conception of Jesus is so crucial to what follows that it is worth asking sceptics some questions:

• Why did the early church invent such a fable, knowing that it would invite a storm of ridicule and contempt? The Jews would reject it because of their high regard for pre-marital chastity, and the Gentiles would be likely to dismiss the whole thing as some kind of dirty joke.

• Why should the writers try to outdo grotesque pagan birth stories with something just as likely to deter recruits?
• Why did a medical practitioner such as Luke risk his reputation by giving the story his endorsement?
• Why was the story not left out of any of the early Christian creeds? Surely someone would have suggested dropping such an embarrassing item from their manifesto?
• Why is there no straightforward record of the birth of Jesus which denies the virgin conception?
• Why has the church always treated Mary with such reverence (some even going to the unbiblical lengths of worshipping her) if she was no more than a common-or-garden fornicator?

The Bible's record is clear and has never been successfully contested: Jesus entered the world in a uniquely miraculous way.

5.
Before the beginning

Many years ago I worked in the Registrar-General's office on the Channel Island of Guernsey, where I shared the responsibility of entering the details of new-born children on the island's official Register of Births. Living on such a small island, I was often aware of impending births long before the proud parent brought the doctor's certificate into the office — but obviously never for more than about nine months. Indications that Jesus was on the way were made somewhat earlier — 2,000 years earlier!

What lies behind this amazing fact? From the time when it first appeared in writing, the Old Testament was never seen by the Jews as just a record of their nation's history, or a collection of man-made religious writings, but as the Word of God, with final authority in all matters of faith and practice. They also recognized it as having one central, unifying theme — God's dealings with mankind in general and with their nation, his chosen people, in particular.[51] Woven into this was God's promise that at some point in time he would break into human history in the form of someone who would fulfil to perfection the three great roles of prophet, priest and king, meet people's deepest spiritual needs and establish God's righteous reign on earth. This great ruler and deliverer came to be known as 'the Anointed One'. The English translation of the Hebrew title is 'Messiah', while the New Testament Greek equivalent, *ho christos*, is 'the Christ'. One prophet after another spoke about his coming, with the last of them, Malachi, summing up God's promise by announcing, 'The messenger of the covenant, whom you desire, will come.'[52] That was God's last word on the subject for 400 years, during which time all the Messianic prophecies remained unfulfilled.

Everything changed when Jesus appeared on the scene. Invited to read the Scriptures as he was worshipping in his local synagogue one day, he deliberately chose a passage in which the prophet Isaiah foretold a day when the Messiah would say,

> The Spirit of the LORD is on me,
>> because he has anointed me
>> to preach good news to the poor.
> He has sent me to proclaim freedom for the
>>> prisoners
>> and recovery of sight for the blind,
> to release the oppressed,
>> to proclaim the year of the Lord's favour.[53]

Listeners who knew their Old Testament had heard these words many times. The nation had been waiting 400 years for their fulfilment, and the synagogue service would normally have proceeded as planned, but what happened next was electrifying:

> Then he rolled up the scroll, gave it back to the attendant and sat down. The eyes of everyone in the synagogue were fastened on him, and he began by saying to them, 'Today this scripture is fulfilled in your hearing.' [54]

What a bombshell! Jesus was claiming that when the prophets wrote about the Messiah they were writing about him, and in the weeks and months that followed Jesus stepped up his insistence that this was the case.

This soon put him in conflict with the religious establishment, especially the Pharisees and the Sadducees, two groups with a special interest in preserving the status quo, but if they thought that they could pressurize Jesus into softening or abandoning his claim they were mistaken. It was not long before he was drawing on all three sections of the Old Testament — the Law, the Poetical Books and the Prophets — to press home his message. Speaking to a group of religious leaders, he commended them for their study of the Old Testament but condemned them for failing to see its meaning: 'You diligently study the Scriptures because you think that by them you possess eternal life. *These are the Scriptures that testify about me*, yet you refuse to come to me to have life.' [55] He told his enemies that their opposition was in fulfilment of a psalm in which the Messiah says, 'They hated me without reason.' [56] When persecution reached the point at which his enemies began plotting to kill him, he referred them to Moses, their great Old Testament lawgiver, and told them point-blank, 'If you believed Moses, you would believe me, for he wrote about me.'[57] Nor did he make any bones about assuming Messianic titles. Knowing that the prophet Daniel had spoken of the Messiah as 'one like a son of man',[58] Jesus deliberately referred to himself as 'the Son of Man' no fewer than seventy-eight times.[59] Yet over the centuries there has been no shortage of charlatans who have made ridiculous claims to have a special place in God's purposes. Could Jesus be one of them? Why should we believe *his* claim to fame?

About 2,000 years before Jesus was born, God told Abraham, the founder of the Jewish nation, that through his offspring, 'All nations on earth will be blessed.'[60] This means that twenty centuries before Jesus was born every other family on earth except Abraham's was out of the running as far as producing the Messiah was concerned. Other Old Testament prophecies showed that Abraham's line of succession would run through Isaac (who was not Abraham's oldest son), Jacob (who was not Isaac's first-born) and Jacob's fourth son Judah (bypassing his eleven brothers). Eleven generations later a man called Jesse was identified as being in the Messianic line, and of Jesse's eight sons David was the one of whom God said that he would 'raise up ... a righteous Branch'.[61]

In a nutshell, then, the Old Testament said that the Messiah would come from a line taken directly through Abraham, Isaac, Jacob, Judah, Jesse and David. This family tree would itself preclude most of the human race, but there were two other significant pointers. One of the Messianic prophecies said that the tribe of Judah would provide Israel with all its kings *until the Messiah arrived*: 'The sceptre will not depart from Judah ... until he comes to whom it belongs'[62] — and Jesus was born just before Judah's government collapsed with the destruction of Jerusalem in A.D.70. The second pointer was the prophecy which told exactly *where* Jesus would be born:

> But you, Bethlehem Ephrathah,
>   though you are small among the clans of Judah,
> out of you will come for me
>   one who will be ruler over Israel. [63]

There were two Bethlehems, one in the region of Ephrathah in Judea, and the other seventy miles to the north in Zebulon: the New Testament tells us that 'Jesus was born in Bethlehem in Judea',[64] the one identified by the Old Testament prophet.

Even this may not be very convincing to the determined sceptic. A student once told me that when Jesus realized he had been born in Bethlehem, and in a family descended from David, he decided to stake a claim to fame by fulfilling all the other Messianic prophecies. This idea is hardly original, and less than persuasive. The nineteenth-century Oxford scholar Henry Liddon traced no fewer than 332 Old Testament prophecies fulfilled by Jesus. These covered his family's social status, his lifestyle, his general demeanour, his teaching and his extraordinary powers. Even more amazingly, they included minute details of the events surrounding his death. The prophets said that he would be forsaken by his followers, betrayed for thirty pieces of silver (which would then be used to buy a potter's field), wrongly accused, tortured and humiliated (in response to which he would not retaliate), executed alongside common criminals, and put to death by crucifixion (a form of execution never carried out by the Jews). They also said that at the time of his death he would pray for his executioners, none of his bones would be broken, his body would be pierced and people would cast lots to see who would get his clothing.

As we can read for ourselves, every one of these things happened, but is it seriously suggested that Jesus would (or could) have 'fixed' all these details to prove his claim to be the Messiah? Peter Stoner evaluated the biblical data using scientific principles of probability, and at one point calculated the chance of just forty-eight of the Messianic prophecies being fulfilled as one in 10^{157}. To illustrate what this means, he used an electron, something so small that, at the rate of 250 a minute, one cubic inch of electrons would take 190,000,000 x 190,000,000 x 190,000,000 years to count. Stoner said that if we took this number of electrons, marked one of them, stirred them all together and then asked a blindfolded friend to find the one we had marked, his chance of doing so would be the same as that of finding one man fulfilling even forty-eight of the more than 300 Messianic prophecies. In Jesus' case, all forty-eight (and another 284) were fulfilled to the letter. Not surprisingly, Stoner concluded that to reject the Bible's claims that Jesus is the Messiah would be to reject a fact 'proved perhaps more absolutely than any other fact in the world'. As he called the quantity of electrons used in his illustration 'a large number', we can hardly accuse him of being prone to exaggeration!

Of the hundreds of Messianic prophecies, let me pinpoint just one more. About 700 years before Jesus was born, the prophet Isaiah promised Ahaz, the eleventh king of Judah, 'Therefore the Lord himself will give you a sign: The virgin will be with child and will give birth to a son.'[65] Sceptics have objected that Isaiah's word for 'virgin' (the Hebrew *almah*) could simply mean 'young woman' and that, if he had wanted to make her virginity clear, he would have used the word *bethulah*. However, this argument has three major weaknesses. In the first place, another prophet uses *bethulah* to describe someone grieving for her husband (and therefore by implication not a virgin).[66] Secondly, the Septuagint (the first Greek translation of the Old Testament) always translates *almah* as *parthenos*, a word which can only mean 'virgin', and as the Septuagint dates from around 300 years *before* Jesus was born, sceptics can hardly say that it was falsified to accommodate his birth. Thirdly, of the nine occasions in which the word *almah* is used in the Old Testament, it is not once clearly used of a woman who is not in fact a virgin. Isaiah's prophecy is clear; Jesus' fulfilment of it is beyond question.

6.
Ten out of ten

Nobody's character and behaviour have been subjected to such intense and relentless scrutiny as those of Jesus, and one of the most surprising things to notice when we read what people have said about him is that some of the greatest tributes have come from the most unexpected sources. Four examples from the nineteenth century, when critical thinking was in full flow in Britain and Europe, will illustrate what I mean.

William Lecky was a famous British historian and strongly sceptical about religion, yet he said that the life of Jesus was 'not only the highest pattern of virtue, but the strongest incentive to its practice'.

The ultra-liberal German theologian David Strauss tried to debunk most of the Bible and denied that Jesus was the Messiah, yet he called him 'the highest object we can possibly imagine with respect to religion, the being without whose presence in the mind piety is impossible'.

The British philosopher John Stuart Mill was one of the century's keenest minds. His ideas were far removed from biblical teaching, yet he wrote of Jesus as 'the ideal representative and guide of humanity'.

The French philosopher and humanist Ernest Renan said, 'Jesus was the greatest religious genius that ever lived. His beauty is eternal and his reign will never end. He is in every respect unique and nothing can be compared with him.'

These are stunning character references, and the Bible shows why they could be given. When a New Testament writer says that Jesus' life was an 'example',[67] the word he uses is *hupogrammos*, which literally means 'writing under'. It was used of words given for children to copy, at times by tracing over the letters the teacher had written. What kind of example did Jesus set? We saw in an earlier chapter that he was a man of prayer and personal devotion, but the New Testament reveals much more. His humility was remarkable: in spite of his unique position and achievements he could say, 'I am not seeking glory for myself.'[68] He was constantly concerned about other people's needs: while others were eaten up with their own interests, he was able to say, 'I am among you as one who serves.'[69] Although he was often misunderstood, wrongly criticized and frequently under pressure from ruthless enemies, he remained 'gentle and humble in heart'[70] and bore no resentment against those who slanderously attacked him. In addition to these qualities, his biography shows him to have been a man of great love, compassion, gentleness, courage, perseverance and faith.

This all paints an impressive picture, yet many other men and women have been extravagantly praised after they have died. A monument in Ripon Cathedral bears this inscription: 'To the memory of William Weddell, Esq., of Newby, in whom every virtue that ennobles the human mind was united with every elegance that adorns it, this monument, a faint emblem of his refined taste, is dedicated by his widow.' Mrs Weddell had obviously been struck by her husband's qualities, but even at her most generous she would not have been able to match the New Testament's statement about Jesus which says that, although he was 'tempted in every way, just as we are', he 'was *without sin*'.[71] This alone sets Jesus apart from every other human being in history, and the evidence to back it up comes from at least five unusual sources.

1. His enemies admitted it

Not all of them did, of course, and in chapter 3 we noted some of the unjustified criticism levelled at him. Yet in the few hours before his death a very different picture emerged. Despite heavy pressure from religious authorities who had hauled Jesus before him on a trumped-up accusation, the Roman governor Pontius Pilate had to admit, 'I find no basis for a charge against him.'[72] While the trial was in progress, Pilate's wife warned him, 'Don't have anything to do with that innocent man, for I have suffered a great deal today in a dream because of him.'[73] We have no details or explanation of the dream, but perhaps Pilate had discussed the case with his wife, and the possibility of her husband being responsible for the execution of an innocent man had been playing on her mind.

Then we have the confession of Judas Iscariot, who had been bribed to betray Jesus to the authorities. When

Jesus was condemned to death, Judas was suddenly 'seized with remorse and returned the thirty silver coins to the chief priests and the elders. "I have sinned," he said, "for I have betrayed innocent blood." '[74] Having been in Jesus' company for three years, with every opportunity to judge his character, Judas could not live with his own conscience, and his subsequent suicide underlines the truth of his testimony.

Next comes a statement from one of the two criminals executed alongside Jesus. At one stage, they both hurled insults at him, but one of them suddenly changed tack. Perhaps remembering some of the things that had been said about Jesus, one of the men cried, 'Aren't you the Christ? Save yourself and us!'[75] His partner could not go along with this: ' "Don't you fear God," he said, "since you are under the same sentence? We are punished justly, for we are getting what our deeds deserve. But this man has done nothing wrong." '[76] The particular phrase he used means, 'He never put a foot out of place.'

Finally, immediately after Jesus died, the Roman army officer in charge of the execution cried out, 'Surely this was a righteous man.'[77] The interesting thing here is that the word 'righteous' means more than 'good'; it means 'upright in the sight of God'. Coming from a hardened professional soldier, no doubt familiar with the way criminals died, this was an astonishing statement.

2. *His followers believed it*

The clearest example is the apostle Paul (originally known as Saul of Tarsus). In his early days, Saul was a strictly orthodox Pharisee, conscientious in his observance of Jewish ceremonial law and an avid student of the Old Testament. Yet he was so bitterly opposed to Jesus and his followers that he began a personal crusade to destroy the early Christian movement. At one stage we find him 'breathing out murderous threats against the Lord's disciples'[78] and getting official permission to arrest them and 'take them as prisoners to Jerusalem'.[79] But something happened to this brilliant, highly educated and powerfully connected man. Having once believed that Jesus was a blasphemous impostor, he was eventually prepared to stake his life on his conviction that Jesus 'had no sin'.[80]

Other New Testament writers came to the same conclusion. The writer of Hebrews summed it up by saying that Jesus was 'holy, blameless, pure, set apart from sinners'[81] and that he 'offered himself unblemished to God'.[82] It is important to realize that in holding to these beliefs these early followers of Jesus were putting their own lives on the line. Paul, for example, was flogged, tortured, imprisoned, stoned, beaten up and, in his own words, 'exposed to death again and again',[83] yet he never flinched from his conviction that his early assessment had been totally mistaken and that, far from being a blasphemous fake, Jesus had been without sin of any kind.

3. *Those who knew him best confirmed it*

Sceptics may say that these people never actually met Jesus, but just ran with a romantic idea to which they were attracted. This hardly explains their willingness to die for their beliefs, but let us listen to his closest friends, who knew him well. His 'inner circle' — Peter, James and John — were with him continually for about three years, in public and in private, in times of popularity and persecution. They had over a thousand days in which to make an accurate assessment, so they were certainly not depending on hearsay, or buying into somebody else's ideas. What did they make of him?

Peter said that Jesus was 'without blemish and defect'[84] and later wrote that 'He committed no sin, and no deceit was found in his mouth.'[85] That second testimony is particularly significant, as the New Testament tells us that Peter himself had previously been guilty of bragging and lying. It seems as if his own weakness in this area made the purity and integrity of Jesus' speech all the more impressive to him.

What makes John's testimony so important is that he describes himself five times as 'the disciple whom Jesus loved'.[86] This obviously refers to a particularly close relationship, which would have given him a unique opportunity to assess his character. What is John's verdict? In one passage alone he calls him 'pure'[87] and 'righteous'[88] and says that in him he saw 'no sin'.[89] As the word 'righteous' is the same as that used by the Roman soldier and means 'upright in the sight of God', the assessment of someone so uniquely well placed to judge could hardly be more convincing. Our closest friends are those most likely to know our weaknesses as well as our strengths; Jesus' closest friends saw no weaknesses.

4. He himself claimed it

The next piece of evidence for the sinlessness of Jesus is in one sense even more remarkable: he himself claimed it. This takes the evidence into a totally new dimension. Do you know of anybody else in history who has credibly made such a claim? Not even the Bible's greatest heroes did so. Israel's King David acknowledged, 'I have sinned greatly.'[90] The prophet Isaiah admitted, 'I am a man of unclean lips.'[91] Job, identified as the most upright man of his day, cried out, 'I despise myself and repent in dust and ashes.'[92] Throughout history, we find similar confessions of failure. Augustine (354-430), one of the greatest theologians the world has ever known, wrote of his 'foulness' and of the 'carnal corruptions of my soul'. John Wesley, whose preaching was an important factor in changing the moral and spiritual climate in eighteenth-century Britain, said on his deathbed, 'I the chief of sinners am.' His contemporary Jonathan Edwards, who was possibly the finest theologian and philosopher America had ever produced, and was once described as 'one of the most holy, humble and heavenly-minded men the world has seen since the apostolic age', said that as far as he was concerned the wickedness of his heart looked 'like an abyss infinitely deeper than hell'. No wonder the Bible says, 'If we claim to be without sin, we deceive ourselves and the truth is not in us.'[93] We may be able to fool some people some of the time, but that is about as far as we can get! Jesus presents a totally different picture. He showed no personal consciousness of sin, and emphasized his sin-lessness in three specific ways.

Speaking of his relationship with God, he said quite openly, 'I always do what pleases him.'[94] His words could hardly have been more specific: he claimed to please God, not sometimes, but 'always'; not in some things, but in everything. Do you know of anyone else in history who could seriously make such a claim?

Jesus also indicated his innocence by separating himself from his hearers when speaking about sin. In giving an illustration about prayer he said, 'If you, then, though you are evil, know how to give good gifts to your children...'[95] Any normal speaker would be expected to say, 'If *we*, then, though *we* are evil...' Then why did Jesus speak of 'you' and not 'we'? Only one explanation fits: he was claiming that, although the lives of all his hearers were polluted by sin, his was not. Again, when teaching what we know as the Lord's Prayer, which includes the petition, 'Forgive us our debts' (that is, our sins),[96] he introduced it by saying, 'This ... is how *you* should pray',[97] not, 'This is how *we* should pray.'

Thirdly, Jesus claimed complete mastery over temptation. While acknowledging the devil's great power and influence, he added, 'He has no hold on me.'[98] Although the devil threw everything at him, Jesus claimed to have remained totally unscathed and unstained. He never blushed with shame, never had a guilty conscience, never regretted anything he said, thought or did, never had any need to apologize, and never asked or prayed for forgiveness. Do you know of anyone else of whom these things could be said?

5. God himself stated it

His enemies admitted it, his followers believed it, his closest friends noticed it and he himself claimed it. This all adds up to striking evidence for the sinlessness of Jesus, but the New Testament adds one clinching factor: God himself stated it. Two of the most significant events in the life of Jesus were his baptism and his transfiguration (a unique and miraculous occasion when his appearance glowed with light). Both were marked by a phenomenon not repeated anywhere else in the Gospel narrative: God spoke from heaven in a voice which could be heard on earth. At his baptism, the words were directed to Jesus: 'You are my Son, whom I love; *with you I am well pleased.*'[99] At the transfiguration they were addressed to Peter, James and John, who were there at the time: 'This is my Son, whom I love; *with him I am well pleased.*'[100] The Bible's verdict on the rest of humanity is that 'All have sinned and fall short of the glory of God,'[101] yet we are told that in the case of Jesus, God was 'well pleased'. The words mean much more than pleasure at someone else's performance (such as parents might have when their child passes an examination). Instead, they imply that Jesus was everything his heavenly Father wanted him to be and that he fulfilled to perfection every part of God's plan for his life. Is that true of anyone you know?

But what about ...?

You would think that such an accumulation of evidence would be enough to convince people that Jesus was without sin, but there can be something uncomfortable about knowing that another human being has succeeded where we have failed, and we should not be too surprised that sceptics have been at work, poring over the New Testament's record of the life of Jesus in the hope of finding a flaw somewhere. As far as I know, they have come up with just three charges that are even worth considering.

1. The cleansing of the temple

The first alleges that Jesus lost his temper when he drove people out of the temple at Jerusalem. The temple was the focal point of Jewish religion, and thousands flocked there, particularly for special events. The Old Testament laid down very strict quality control for sacrifices to be offered at the temple, but officials and others found ways of working the system to their advantage. A farmer might bring his best cow or sheep, only for an inspector to rule it unacceptable. This forced the farmer to buy a replacement from a vendor (who was in collusion with the inspector) operating a nearby concession. Anxious to get to worship, the farmer would pay up and the inspector and the vendor would both get their agreed share of the profits. People who could not afford to sacrifice animals were allowed to bring doves, but the same kind of shady deal operated at the lower end of the market. Money-changers were also on to a good thing. Every Jew had to pay an annual temple tax, but it could be paid only in certain specified currencies. Needless to say, *bureaux de change* were on the spot, delighted to oblige — and to pocket an extortionate commission.

This was too much for Jesus, and he drove the swindlers out, telling them that whereas God had called the temple 'a house of prayer' they had turned it into 'a den of robbers'.[102] Was Jesus angry? Yes, he was. Did he sin? No! Far from condemning all anger, the Bible actually *commands* it, but with one important condition: 'Be angry, and yet do not sin.'[103] There is a difference between unrighteous and righteous anger. Anger which is unjustified, bitter, self-serving, 'over the top', or motivated by sin of any kind, is obviously wrong, but there is clearly such a thing as righteous anger. When I hear of a ninety-year-old woman being brutally raped, I am angry. When I hear of children being molested, I am angry. When I read of hard-pressed, elderly householders being exploited by unscrupulous workmen, I am angry. Anybody who hears about terrorism, violence, sadism and robbery *should* be angry. There is something radically wrong with people who can shrug their shoulders at injustice and 'man's inhumanity to man'. The Bible tells us that God 'expresses his wrath every day'.[104] In the very nature of things, God's anger must be both holy and justifiable; Jesus can hardly be criticized for expressing exactly the same emotion.

2. The withering of the fig tree

The second charge is along the same lines, and stems from the following incident:

> Early in the morning, as he was on his way back to the city, [Jesus] was hungry. Seeing a fig tree by the road, he went up to it but found nothing on it except leaves. Then he said to it, 'May you never bear fruit again!' Immediately the tree withered. [105]

This seems a much stronger case — but is it? Although the time of year (around mid-April) was too early for full-grown figs, there should have been little edible knobs called *taqsh*. However, this particular tree had 'nothing on it except leaves', a sure sign that it was diseased in some way and would not bear any fruit that year. Jesus' response was not to rant and rave, lose his temper or attack the tree, like John Cleese venting his spleen on his car in a classic episode of *Fawlty Towers*. Instead, he simply said, 'May you never bear fruit again!' and the tree withered and died. This certainly shows that Jesus was someone *special*, but how does it show that he was *sinful*? Do we think that people who cut down trees in their gardens are doing something wrong?

The Bible often uses the fig tree as a symbol of God's chosen nation of Israel, and this incident was obviously meant as a parable. God intended Israel to be spiritually fruitful but its religious system had become thoroughly corrupt and could be said to have 'nothing on it except leaves'. In doing what he did to the fig tree, Jesus was forecasting the downfall of Israel and the coming of a time when (as he told those who saw what had happened) 'the kingdom of God will be taken away from you and given to a people who will produce its fruit'.[106] This prophecy was fulfilled in the passing away of the old order and the foundation of the Christian church.

What Jesus did was certainly miraculous, but there is no way in which it could be called malicious. If I thought that the weeds in my garden would wither and die if I told them to, I would not feel in the least bit guilty about having a word with them! Case dismissed.

3. *The conversation with the rich young ruler*

The third charge centres around a conversation Jesus had with a wealthy young man:

> As Jesus started on his way, a man ran up to him and fell on his knees before him. 'Good teacher,' he asked, 'what must I do to inherit eternal life?' 'Why do you call me good?' Jesus answered. 'No one is good — except God alone.'[107]

The allegation here is that in saying, 'No one is good — except God alone', Jesus was admitting that he himself was *not* good, in other words that he too was a sinner. On the face of it, this sounds like a fair charge, but does it stand up? If so, it contradicts every other statement Jesus made about his own character because, as we saw earlier, he repeatedly claimed to live a life that was perfect in every way. A sudden contradiction at this point makes no sense.

However, the case collapses when we notice that the conversation was not about Jesus' character at all, but about that of the other man. By calling Jesus 'Good teacher', he was not making a judgement on Jesus' character, any more than 'Dear Sir' at the beginning of a letter implies a deep sense of affection. Jesus shrewdly took up the man's use of the word 'good' and, having drawn his attention to the character of God, reminded him of the six commandments which refer to human relationships: 'Do not murder, do not commit adultery, do not steal, do not give false testimony, do not defraud, honour your father and mother.'[108] Without batting an eyelid, the young man replied, 'All these I have kept since I was a boy.'[109] He obviously thought that he *was* good, but his reply showed that he had no idea that God's law extended beyond actions to thoughts, affections and desires. When Jesus responded by telling him to sell all his possessions and give the proceeds to the poor, 'The man's face fell,' and he 'went away sad, because he had great possessions'.[110] This showed his goodness to be selective and superficial. It also showed that he was addicted to his wealth, breaking the very first commandment: 'You shall have no other gods before me.'[111]

Even this brief outline of the incident makes it clear that *it had nothing to do with the character of Jesus*. The young man never referred to it, nor did Jesus himself.

Instead, the story is meant to show us that none of man's attempts at being 'good' can ever measure up to God's requirements, and that we cannot get right with God by our own efforts.

After scouring every word in the New Testament for about 2,000 years, critics and sceptics of every kind have come up with just three charges against the character of Jesus, not one of which is worth taking to court. Instead, all the evidence we have points to a man whose character is unique in human culture. He is not merely the finest; he is flawless; and the more we read of his life, the more we see that all of his matchless qualities were held in perfect balance. After many years of painstaking study, the modern British author Robert Clarke came to this conclusion: 'There was meekness without weakness; tenderness without feebleness; firmness without coarseness; love without sentimentality; holiness without sanctimoniousness; lowliness without lowness; truth without error; enthusiasm without fanaticism; passion without prejudice; heavenly-mindedness without forgetfulness; carefreeness without carelessness; service without servility; self-exaltation without egotism; judgement without harshness; seriousness without sombreness; mercy without softness.'

Faced one day with some of his most relentless critics, Jesus asked, 'Can any of you prove me guilty of sin?'[112] Nobody could — or can.

7.
Mission accomplished

It is fascinating to discover what some people think is the main purpose or achievement of their lives. Some years ago, Associated Newspapers ran the story of an eighty-eight-year-old British peer who had devoted his life to breeding the perfect spotted mouse. During a visit I once paid to Greece, the local press announced the death of a well-known bishop of the Greek Orthodox Church, and praised him to the skies for his greatest achievement: he had master-minded the removal of the bones of St Andrew from Italy to Greece.

Other people are noted for accomplishments far more significant than mating rodents or moving remains. Political influence, philosophical ideas, military leadership, scientific discovery, social reform and medical skill are some of the things for which people are remembered centuries after their time. Then of all that was done by the person at the heart of Y2K, which was the most important thing? The Bible's answer is amazing: *he died*.

This is reflected in the fact that the universally recognized symbol of the movement he began is not a reminder

of his unique conception, his sinless character, his unequalled teaching, or his remarkable miracles (we will look
at these in chapter 9), but a *cross*, the cruellest instru-
ment of execution known to the ancient world, and one
which has been banned for the last 1,500 years. On the
face of it, this seems bizarre, if not grotesque. What other
leader is instantly associated with a guillotine, an electric
chair, a noose, or a poison phial? Can we imagine minia-
tures of these things decorating buildings, stamped on
religious books or worn as jewellery? The mystery deep-
ens when we realize that the cross was grossly offensive
to the three major cultures of Jesus' day. The Roman
statesman and orator Cicero wrote, 'Even the mere word
"cross" must remain far not only from the lips of the citi-
zens of Rome, but also from their thoughts, their eyes,
their ears.' To the Jews, anybody hanging on a cross was
said to be under God's curse,[113] while the Greeks thought
that attaching any significance to the death of Jesus was
'absurd and utterly unphilosophical nonsense'.[114]

Yet when we read the New Testament it is obvious
that what dominates its pages is not the life of Jesus but
his death. It has been calculated that about 40% of the
Gospel of Matthew, 60% of the Gospel of Mark, over
30% of the Gospel of Luke and nearly 50% of the Gospel
of John are taken up with the events leading up to and
surrounding the moment when he was crucified. There is
the same kind of emphasis in the rest of the New Testament. The apostle Paul, who wrote more of it than anyone else, summed up his message in one phrase: 'We
preach Christ crucified.'[115] After working in Corinth for

eighteen months, he reminded his friends there, 'I resolved to know nothing while I was with you except Jesus Christ and him crucified.'[116]

It is equally obvious that Jesus saw his death as *central* to his life, and not as the event which ended it. When he was catapulted into the limelight at the beginning of his public ministry he said, 'My time has not yet come.'[117] Later, two life-threatening situations were defused 'because his time had not yet come',[118] but a few days before his death his language suddenly changed. When Greek visitors to Jerusalem asked to see him, he said, 'The hour has come for the Son of Man to be glorified,' and 'It was for this very reason I came to this hour.'[119] Then, on the night of his arrest, he prayed, 'Father, the time has come.'[120] As far as Jesus was concerned, his death was to be the climax of his life, not merely its conclusion. As the modern British scholar John Stott puts it, 'The hour for which he had come into the world was the hour in which he left it.'

Why should that be the case? What is so special about the death of Jesus? It has nothing to do with the method used to execute him. Alexander the Great once crucified a thousand of his enemies, certain Persian rulers were known to use the threat of crucifixion to deter rebellion and the Romans crucified countless provincial insurgents. There was certainly nothing unusual about crucifixion in those days; after all, Jesus was one of a batch of three men crucified simultaneously.

The mere fact that Jesus died seems anything but remarkable. After all, death is universal and inescapable. It has been said that the whole world is a hospital, and every person in it a terminal patient. Nobody has to ask, 'Is there death after life?', because the simple fact is that what we call 'living' could just as accurately be called 'dying'. Yet everybody should surely ask another question: *why?* Why should every one of us have to accept the fact that, as a friend of mine once put it, 'We are not here to stay; we are here to go'? No matter how much attention we lavish on these bodies of ours, they will be nothing more than fertilizer in a few years' time. People who never find themselves asking, 'Why?' are simply not thinking seriously. Why is death a fact of life? What is it that causes us to die? Why should we not go on living here on earth for ever?

In the course of my work in the Registrar-General's office I wrote out hundreds of death certificates, and can still remember the strange emotion I often felt when completing the column headed 'Cause of Death'. Sometimes, the words I had to write were frighteningly long — 'arteriosclerotic degeneration of the myocardium' — while at other times a chilling word like 'cancer' said it all. Yet even when we have waded through an encyclopaedia of diseases, we have only discovered *how* people die. To answer the deeper question, 'Why?', we have to turn back to the Bible.

The intruder

The first mention of death comes very early in the Bible, *but not at the beginning*. Man was originally created 'in the image of God',[121] morally and spiritually perfect, and in complete harmony with his Creator. Yet this state of affairs was dependent on our first parents' total and un-qualified obedience, and God warned them that should they ever disobey they would 'surely die'.[122] Some time later they did disobey — yet they went on living for many years. The explanation of this conundrum is so important that if I could write it here in letters six feet high I would do so: *the basic meaning of 'death' is not termination but separation*. The Bible speaks of both physical and spiritual death; the first is the separation of the soul from the body and the second is the separation of the soul from God. This is the vital clue to understanding what hap-pened to Adam and Eve, the world's first two human beings. The moment they sinned, they died spiritually; their relationship with God was shattered. What is more, from the moment of their first sin, their bodies became subject to disease, decay and deterioration and eventu-ally they died physically. God's penalty for sin had been carried out in full, and to the letter.

What links that piece of ancient history to me as I write these words, and to you as you read them, is that it was *after* he had become polluted by sin that Adam began to father children, and that he then did so '*in his own like-ness, in his own image*'.[123] From then on, like poison dumped at the source of a river, Adam's corrupt nature has flowed down to every generation since. Today, trendy thinking pokes fun at the idea of what theologians call 'original sin', but it is the only explanation of the kind of behaviour that plagues modern society. (It even explains why some people ridicule the Bible's clear teaching on the subject!)

On one occasion, Jesus gave examples of the kind of behaviour I have in mind — evil thoughts, murder, adultery, sexual immorality, theft, false testimony and slander — and he made it clear that these all come from 'the heart'.[124] This kind of behaviour does not *make* people sinners; it proves they already *are* sinners. Certain kinds of behaviour may be more prevalent under certain social conditions, but the bottom line is that anything that comes short of the perfect obedience to his law which God deserves, desires and demands comes from corrupt human nature. We do not become sinners because we sin; we sin because we are sinners, caught up in the flow of Adam's fall. It was a realization of this that led the American novelist Mark Twain to say, 'If man should be crossed with the cat, it would improve man, but it would deteriorate the cat'!

The answer to the question 'Why do we die?' is that death (physical and spiritual) is the outworking of what the Bible calls 'the law of sin and death';[125] one leads directly and inevitably to the other. But if that is the case, *why did Jesus die?* The reason why we need to ask this question is obvious. As Jesus had no sin of any kind, and it is sin which causes death, he clearly had no 'cause of death' in him. Because he was sinless, he was not subject to the law of sin and death. He was outside of its jurisdiction. Yet he died! What is the answer to this massive mystery? The Bible's response is to say that the death of Jesus was unique in two ways.

The death that was different

In the first place, it remains the only voluntary death in human history. Death is not an option for any of us; in the Bible's own words, we are all 'destined to die'.[126] Whatever plans we may make for our lives, the last item is already on the agenda: death. But what about those who lose their lives trying to rescue others, or servicemen killed in acts of bravery against overwhelming odds? None of these *chooses* to die. The most we can say is that they risk dying sooner than they otherwise might. Not even suicides decide to die; they merely choose the day, the time, the place and the method.

Jesus went one massive step further. Although death had no claim on him, he made it clear that he would deliberately submit to it in a way that meant something very different from suicide: 'No one takes [my life] from me, but I lay it down of my own accord.'[127] When Jesus was arrested, one of his followers attacked a high priest's servant and hacked off his ear, but Jesus told him to put his sword away and said, 'Do you think I cannot call on my Father, and he will at once put at my disposal more than twelve legions of angels?'[128] As a Roman legion consisted of 7,000 soldiers and the Old Testament tells of one angel killing 185,000 soldiers in a single night, twelve legions of angels would have been capable of wiping out more than the entire population of the world at that time. Yet Jesus was going beyond mathematics and making it clear that, although he could have escaped from any size of arresting party at any time he wished, *he chose not to do so*.

Another piece of evidence comes at the very moment
he died: 'And when Jesus had cried out again in a loud
voice, *he gave up his spirit*.'[129] The literal meaning of the
phrase I have emphasized is, 'He sent his spirit away,'
like a manager dismissing a workman. The significance
of this is that the Bible specifically states, 'No one has
power over the day of his death.'[130] If a man could prevent the spirit leaving his body, he could make himself
immortal, and if he could dismiss his spirit by an act of
the will, suicide would be simple and serene. Yet once
again, Jesus is the exception to the rule. He deliberately,
clearly and intelligently dismissed his spirit; he told it to
go. He was not drugged (he had refused the crude anaes-
thetic offered to him),[131] nor was he totally exhausted (he
had the strength to cry out 'in a loud voice').[132] Instead,
he showed that he had complete authority over the entire
process of dying, including the precise moment of his
death. As Augustine wrote some 400 years later, 'He gave
up his life *because* he willed it, *when* he willed and *as* he
willed it.'

In the second place, the death of Jesus remains the
only one experienced *on behalf of others and in their
place*. We are all moved by stories of those who sacrifice
their lives to rescue others from danger, but what Jesus
did was in a different league altogether: he took upon
himself the death penalty for sin which others deserved.
Old Testament prophecies had spoken of a suffering servant who would bear the sins of others and die in their
place, and at a last meal with his disciples Jesus quoted
the passage concerned and told them that 'What is written

about me is reaching its fulfilment.'[133] At the same meal, he said that the wine they were drinking was a symbol of his own blood, 'which is poured out for many for the forgiveness of sins'.[134] His meaning was clear: he was to die in the place of others and for their benefit.

Elsewhere in the New Testament we find the same tremendous truth underlined. Paul says, 'Christ died for the ungodly,'[135] and 'While we were still sinners, Christ died for us.'[136] Peter was just as insistent: 'He himself bore our sins in his body on the tree.'[137] So was John: 'Jesus Christ laid down his life for us.'[138] God's perfect holiness demands that all sin — every sin — must be punished, and when Jesus took the place of others he became as accountable for their sins as if he had been responsible for them.

Some people see the death of Jesus as a moving example of how to endure undeserved suffering with meekness, courage and dignity. It certainly *is* an example of that, and one which remains an uncomfortable challenge to each one of us in a world in which submission is out of style and people fight like cats and dogs to assert what they see as their rights. Yet this misses the main point. Jesus did not die to give us a courageous example of how to suffer in silence, nor was his death simply an attempt to win our love or allegiance. Surely that would have been emotional blackmail and ultimately pointless? I would have been less than impressed if, during our honeymoon in northern France, my wife had decided to demonstrate her love for me by throwing herself off the top of Mont St Michel! That would have been a tragic waste

of her life and a terrible blow to mine. Yet everywhere we
look in the Bible we see that the death of Jesus was *not* a
waste. At the time of his transfiguration, Jesus spoke with
others about his death, 'which he was about to *accom-
plish* at Jerusalem'.[139] Notice the word I have emphasized.
Most people think of death as some kind of failure —
such as defeat by a disease, the elements, or a stronger
opponent. Who ever speaks of death as something 'ac-
complished'? Jesus did! Virtually his last words as he hung
on the cross were, 'It is finished.'[140] In New Testament
Greek it is just one word — *tetelesthai* — the word often
written across a bill in those days to show that it had been
paid in full. This was not a cry of despair, but of triumph.
In that one word, Jesus announced that the specific purpose for which he had come into the world was being
fulfilled at that very moment.

The Bible speaks of what the death of Jesus accom-
plished in a number of ways. It says that it was an 'aton-
ing sacrifice',[141] in which he took upon himself the consequences of God's anger against the sins of others and in
so doing turned it away from them and made it possible
for God to act favourably towards them. Secondly, Jesus
himself said that he gave his life 'as a ransom for many'.[142]
By nature and choice people are 'slaves to sin',[143] but Jesus
gave his own life as the ransom price to set them free
from their moral and spiritual slavery. Elsewhere, the Bible
uses another picture to explain what Jesus did in dying on
the cross. It says that people who were God's enemies
were 'reconciled to him through the death of his Son',[144]
and that as a result they have 'peace with God'.[145]

Peter summed it all up by saying, 'Christ died for sins once for all, the just for the unjust, in order that he might bring us to God.'[146] There was no bending of the rules, no back-room deal. God remained holy and just and inflexibly opposed to sin, yet in the life and death of his Son, Jesus Christ, he provided a way in which sinners can get right with God. His holy law makes two demands on us: as God's creatures, we must obey it in every part; as law-breakers, we must pay its penalty in full. In an act of amazing love *Jesus did both*; and he did so on behalf of guilty, lost and helpless sinners such as the person writing this book — and the one reading it.

Only when we grasp this can we begin to understand what the millennium is all about.

8.
Man alive!

Jesus died at three o'clock on a Friday afternoon. Soon
afterwards, a wealthy friend named Joseph, who came
from the town of Arimathea and was a high-profile member of the Jewish Sanhedrin (or Senate) at Jerusalem,
asked if he could remove the body for burial. When the
Roman officer in charge of the execution squad confirmed
that Jesus was dead — a soldier thrust a spear into the
corpse just to make sure — Pontius Pilate gave the necessary permission.

To comply with Jewish law, Joseph and Nicodemus,
another of Jesus' friends, took the body down from the
cross at some time before sunset. After wrapping it in
linen bandages, layered with about thirty-four kilograms
of myrrh and aloes (aromatic spices commonly used for
embalming the dead), they laid it to rest in a cave which
Joseph had previously earmarked as his own tomb, closed
the entrance with a large rock, then went sadly back to
their homes.

If Jesus' followers were distraught, his enemies were
delighted. After three years of attracting controversial

publicity, he had finally been silenced. Now they could get on with running the religious establishment in their own self-serving way, without the risk of Jesus exposing their greed, pride and hypocrisy. Just one thing was niggling them. Jesus had said, 'After three days I will rise again,'[147] apparently suggesting that his death would *not* be the end of the story. This was a ridiculous idea to them, but what if his followers stole the body and then claimed that their leader *had* come back to life? On the following day, they shared their fears with Pontius Pilate and suggested that he knock that possibility on the head by imposing maximum security on the tomb for the next few days. Pilate agreed. Jesus had not merely been a nuisance; there had been signs of his becoming a political menace, so this was no time for half measures. A guard of soldiers was posted with instructions to make the tomb 'as secure as you know how'.[148] Pilate's official seal was attached to the rock covering the entrance and the guards arranged a roster to keep the site under round-the-clock surveillance until the third day had passed. The last chapter in the Jesus saga had apparently been written.

Within forty-eight hours there had been a sensational development: *the body was missing*. Had such a thing happened today, the foreign news media would scarcely have had time to get home before rushing back to Jerusalem. A few hours later, even this news took second place as the city was rocked by a rumour which quickly got out of control: *Jesus had risen from the dead*.

Alternatives

Was the story true or false? As we shall see later, the
implications are so stupendous that no sensible person
can brush the issue aside as being irrelevant. On the original BBC *Brains Trust*, Professor C. E. M. Joad was asked,
'If you could ask one question and be sure of getting the
right answer, what would you ask?' He replied, 'Did Jesus
Christ rise from the dead?' The issue is so crucial that we
need to assess the evidence carefully. Before doing so, it
is worth looking at the alternative theories that have been
put forward.

1. 'The tomb was not empty'

This idea never gets off the ground. At least five people
visited the tomb on the Sunday morning and confirmed
that the body had gone, and there is no contemporary
record of anyone denying it. What is more, within a few
weeks Jesus' followers were putting their lives on the
line by branding his murderers as 'godless men'[149] and
insisting that he had come back to life. If they were lying,
all the authorities had to do was to open the tomb and
invite people to see the body for themselves; the resurrection story would have been killed off within the hour.

2. 'The first visitors went to the wrong tomb'

This theory was first put forward in 1907, but it suffers
from more than old age. Two of them had been present at

the burial just thirty-six hours earlier and 'saw where he was laid'.[150] The word translated 'saw' means 'looked with interest and for a purpose'. Would they really have forgotten what they had seen, *and where they had seen it*? Nor were these eyewitnesses standing a long way off; we are specifically told that they 'saw the tomb *and how his body was laid in it*'.[151] Having taken such a close interest in what had happened (they wanted to return the next day to anoint the dead body according to Jewish custom), would they have completely lost their way back there? Even if this was the case, why did they not ask Joseph for directions? Would this intelligent man have forgotten the location of his own private burial plot, especially when he had been there a day or so earlier to lay a dear friend's body to rest? The 'wrong tomb' idea is absurd.

3. 'The body was stolen by a person or persons unknown'

Tomb robbers were common enough at the time, but there is not a shred of evidence that they had touched this one. What motive could they have had? Why would they leave behind the only things of any commercial value (the grave-clothes and spices) and make off with a naked body? As Sir Norman Anderson says, 'A Jew of that period could scarcely be suspected of stealing bodies on behalf of anatomical research!' It took 500 years for somebody to come up with this idea, but it can be seen off in a few seconds.

4. 'The Roman authorities removed the body'

They obviously had the opportunity to do so, as they were
in charge of the tomb, but it is difficult to see why they
would want to. What would they gain by removing it and
placing it under another guard somewhere else? Again,
when his followers began preaching that Jesus had risen
from the dead, the Romans could in that case have
strangled the whole Christian movement at birth by producing the body. There can be only one reason why they
failed to do so: they had no body to produce.

5. 'The Jewish religious authorities removed the body'

They also had the opportunity, as they were hand in glove
with the Romans and might have suggested that they
would be happy to take over their own countryman's body
for the four days necessary to prove his prophecy wrong.
They also had the motive of quashing the Jesus movement once and for all. What is lacking here is any evidence that this happened, and the theory fails for the same
reason as the previous one. When Jesus' followers began
preaching that he had risen from the dead, why did the
Jewish authorities have them arrested, imprisoned, flogged
and killed, when they could have silenced them by simply
producing the body?

6. 'Jesus' followers removed the body'

Why? What motive would they have had to remove it
from a tomb donated by a prominent member of the

community? As to opportunity, the Jewish religious leaders invented one particular story that was still circulating some twenty years later. The Bible records that the guards at the grave had been shaken by an earthquake, then stunned by the appearance of an angel who rolled away the rock to reveal an empty tomb.[152] It also tells us what happened after the guards reported back to the chief priests: 'When the chief priests had met with the elders and devised a plan, they gave the soldiers a large sum of money, telling them, "You are to say, 'His disciples came during the night and stole him away while we were asleep.' If this report gets to the governor, we will satisfy him and keep you out of trouble." So the soldiers took the money and did as they were instructed.'[153]

It is not difficult to see why this face-saving plan was cobbled together. The guards' report would fit in with a resurrection scenario — with serious implications for those responsible for hounding Jesus to death. Yet the whole thing unravels as soon as we ask some obvious questions. Would hand-picked Roman guards have fallen asleep on duty when the penalty for doing so was execution? Would *every one* of them have nodded off? How did Jesus' followers get into the tomb, break the seal, roll the rock away, remove the grave-clothes and make off with the body, all without disturbing even one of the soldiers? If the guards were asleep, *how would they know who had stolen the body*? Would the disciples have left a visiting card?

An alternative theory has them snatching Jesus' body while the guards were still awake, but this is hopelessly weak. After the crucifixion, these men went into hiding 'with the doors locked for fear of the Jews'.[154] Can we imagine them suddenly plucking up the courage to tackle an armed Roman guard and risk the death penalty by breaking the governor's official seal, all for the sake of removing a body already in the safe keeping of one of their most influential friends? If we can, why is there no record of their ever being charged with the offences involved?

There are other problems with both theories involving Jesus' followers. They had spent three years under the powerful influence of his matchless moral teaching, and were later to write New Testament books reflecting this. Would they be likely to invent a pack of lies as the basis for what they had to say? Nor would the lies have been about minor matters. The apostle Paul (who claimed to have met the risen Jesus some time later) wrote that, if Jesus had not been raised from the dead, 'we are even found to be false witnesses of God, because we witnessed against God that he raised Christ'.[155] Notice carefully what he is saying here. If Jesus was not raised from the dead, his followers were not only claiming to be witnesses of something they knew to be false, *they were attributing to God something they knew perfectly well he had not done.* Yet these were men whose writings showed that they had a passionate concern for God's honour and glory! The whole idea is nonsensical.

This ties in with a serious psychological problem. As soon as these men started preaching that Jesus was alive, they were persecuted by the religious leaders, hauled before the Sanhedrin and given strict instructions to stop doing so. Their response was to declare, 'We must obey God rather than men!'[156] and then to head straight back to the streets. As a result, they were bullied, threatened and flogged, and eventually some of them were executed. Would they have withstood such persecution if they had removed Jesus' body and buried it elsewhere? They might have risked their lives for something they had imagined, *but not for something they had invented.* Men are sometimes prepared to die for convictions, but not for concoctions. One expert after another has examined the evidence in this area and come to the same conclusion: for these men to have buried the body and then risk their lives preaching that Jesus was alive would have been psychologically impossible.

7. 'Jesus never actually died'

This is the so-called 'swoon theory', but it never stands up to the facts. Before releasing the body, Pilate insisted on a death certificate from the officer in charge of the execution, and a soldier had rammed his spear into the corpse to make doubly sure that death had occurred.[157] This alone should make the swoon theory impossible to accept; the scenario it calls for shows it to be pure fantasy. Think of what is being suggested: traumatized by beatings and scourgings and by being nailed to a cross for three hours, Jesus lost consciousness, but remained alive — even after the soldier's spear had ripped open his side. While he was being taken down from the cross, prepared for burial and laid in the tomb, neither Joseph nor

Nicodemus detected any sign of breathing. At some time during the next thirty-six hours (revived by the cold air in the tomb or by the strong-smelling spices?) Jesus came out of coma and, like some first-century Houdini, wriggled his way out of the tightly-wound grave-clothes layered with sticky embalming material. With a baffling recovery of energy he then pushed aside the huge rock blocking the entrance to the tomb, overcame the entire armed guard and (the grave-clothes were left behind) made his way stark naked into the city. Within a few hours, he had made such a remarkable recovery from the terrible trauma and loss of blood that when he met his friends he persuaded them, not that he had somehow stumbled back from the brink of death, but that he had overcome death and burst through into a new and more dynamic life than they had ever experienced. To cap it all, after a lifetime during which he had never committed a single sin, Jesus suddenly became a blatant and blasphemous liar, conning his best friends into believing something which he knew to be false. The swoon theory never gets to its feet.

Facts in favour

If the alternative theories are weak, the evidence for the resurrection of Jesus is powerful and consistent, and is backed up by some unexpected credentials. In the first place, nobody claimed to have seen it happen. But if the disciples had cooked up the story, surely they would have included a dramatic eyewitness account? Secondly, the

Bible says that the first person to see Jesus alive after his resurrection was a woman;[158] yet in those days a woman's testimony was considered almost worthless. Would the disciples have risked compromising their claim by relying on such a flimsy foundation? Thirdly, while the different narratives agree on the essentials, they are not identical, and it is virtually impossible to fit them into a precise chronological order. This may seem like a weakness, but it is exactly the opposite. If the disciples had invented the story, would they not have made sure all the loose ends were tied up? When several reports of a political meeting, a concert or a football match emphasize different points, or mention certain facts in a different order, nobody suggests that the event concerned never happened. The fact that New Testament reports of the resurrection are not identical is a strong point in its favour. Then what of the evidence itself? Out of all the available material, here are three of the most impressive items:

1. The number of witnesses

The Bible records six independent, written testimonies (three of them by eyewitnesses) telling of eleven separate occasions, over a period of forty days, when Jesus appeared to various people. Sceptics have suggested that these 'appearances' were hallucinations, but this attack breaks down because hallucinations conform to certain laws and the resurrection appearances refuse to fit the stereotype. Those to whom Jesus appeared included a number of women,[159] a sceptical brother,[160] several fishermen,[161] a brilliant intellectual[162] and a close friend who was deeply sceptical about the whole thing even when others assured him that they had met the risen Jesus face to face.[163] He appeared in a garden, in a home, on a road-side, out in the country, on the seashore and on a hillside. He appeared at many different times of the day, and hardly ever in places where he and his disciples had spent time together. These facts lead the distinguished medical expert Dr A. Rendle Short to say, 'The resurrection appearances break every known law of visions.'

What is more, Jesus appeared not merely to individuals, but to two, three, seven, eleven and on one occasion over 500 people at the same time. Surely this is an impressive argument? A friend of mine once shocked 200 students at a school assembly by cutting the headmaster's tie in two with a pair of scissors, and then went on to say something like this: 'Imagine that on your way home this afternoon you met a friend and told him that you had seen the assembly speaker chop the headmaster's tie in two. Your friend would probably think that you were pulling his leg, but supposing three other students who were there at the time told him the same story, and then that tomorrow thirty students did so. Now imagine that by the end of the week all 200 students present at the assembly had told your friend the same thing. Would it be reasonable for him to doubt them?'

The Bible's evidence for the resurrection of Jesus is even more impressive. When Paul told friends at Corinth that Jesus appeared to more than five hundred people at the same time, he added, *'most of whom are still living'*.[164] Those who doubted that Jesus had risen from the dead could have quizzed over 250 witnesses, and every one of them would have told the same story. Why should they have done this? And why should hallucinations convince them that Jesus had risen from the dead? After all, resurrection was the last thing they expected; the first women at the tomb went to anoint their friend's remains,[165] not to announce his return at a press conference! Eyewitness testimonies by hundreds of people who saw Jesus after his resurrection are in a different league from the bizarre beliefs of those who say that Elvis Presley is still alive!

Other sceptics suggest that what these hundreds of people saw was some kind of spirit or ghost, but this hardly matches the facts. What about the empty tomb? What do we make of those who 'clasped his feet'[166] when they saw him? What of the occasion when he went into a house with two disciples, 'took bread, gave thanks, broke it and began to give it to them'?[167] What of those who 'ate and drank with him after he rose from the dead'?[168] Are ghosts in the habit of eating and drinking and passing food around? Then there was the incident with the sceptical Thomas, who refused to believe in the resurrection unless he could touch the wounds made in Jesus' body by the nails and spear.[169] A week later, Jesus appeared to him and said, 'Put your finger here; see my hands. Reach out your hand and put it into my side. Stop doubting and believe.'[170] Does this read like a ghost story?

2. The transformation of the disciples

If the physical appearance of Jesus to hundreds of people in different circumstances over a seven-week period is the primary piece of evidence that Jesus rose from the dead, the dramatic change that came over the disciples runs it a close second. As we saw earlier, the crucifixion of Jesus left them a dejected, faithless and demoralized rabble, cowering behind locked doors for fear that they might be next on the authorities' hit list. Yet seven weeks later they came out of hiding, took to the streets and risked their lives by preaching the resurrection of Jesus. What is more, their chief spokesman was Peter. When Jesus was arrested, Peter was so terrified that he swore he never even knew him.[171] Now, not even persecution by the Sanhedrin could stop him, and people were 'astonished'[172] at his courage. What is more, the same change came over all the disciples. Suddenly, they were prepared to face persecution, imprisonment and even execution rather than deny their conviction that Jesus was alive. This tremendous transformation from cowardice to courage leads Sir Norman Anderson to claim that it is 'far and away the strongest circumstantial evidence for the resurrection'.

3. A movement that has gone on growing

The third piece of evidence brings the second one up to date. Within a few years, enemies of Christianity accused its leaders of having 'caused trouble all over the world'.[173] By the early part of the fourth century, the movement was recognized as the official religion of the Roman Empire, which had tried to kill it off at birth. Some 2,000 years later, it is the largest religious movement the world has ever known. But what started it all? It was not a new line in moral teaching, nor an original slant on social issues, nor a trendy new style of worship. One thing sparked off this new movement and fuelled its dynamic growth — *the resurrection of Jesus*. The climax of Peter's first sermon was the claim that 'God has raised this Jesus to life.'[174] When questioned about their miraculous power, the apostles said that they were acting in 'the name of Jesus of Nazareth ... whom God raised from the dead'.[175] The linchpin of New Testament teaching is that Jesus was 'raised on the third day'.[176] The eminent historian Kenneth Scott Latourette says that, but for the disciples' conviction that Jesus had risen from the dead, 'the death of Jesus and even Jesus himself would probably have been all but forgotten'. Yet he is not forgotten. More people than ever before — about 1.6 billion — now claim to share the disciples' belief.

Verdicts

How convincing is the evidence for the resurrection of Jesus? Here are some impressive verdicts to consider:

• In a document found among his private papers, Lord Lyndhurst, one of the greatest minds in British legal history, wrote, 'I know pretty well what evidence is; and I tell you, such evidence as that for the resurrection has never broken down yet.'
• The outstanding Harvard professor Dr Simon Greenleaf, whose work *A Treatise on the Law of Evidence* was considered the greatest of its kind, said of the apostles' transformation, 'It was ... impossible that they

could have persisted in affirming the truths they have narrated, had not Jesus actually risen from the dead, and had they not known this fact as certainly as they knew any other fact.'

• The distinguished legal counsel Sir Edward Clarke, KC, wrote, 'As a lawyer, I have made a prolonged study for the events of the first Easter Day. To me the evidence is conclusive, and over and over again in the High Court I have secured the verdict on evidence not nearly so compelling.'

• Lord Darling, a former Chief Justice of England, said, 'There exists such overwhelming evidence, positive and negative, factual and circumstantial, that no intelligent jury in the world could fail to bring in a verdict that the resurrection story is true.'

Anybody who tosses these opinions aside needs to have convincing reasons for doing so. Accepting that Jesus rose from the dead is ultimately a matter of faith, but it is not a leap in the dark. It is based on powerful and persuasive evidence.

Nor is this the end of the story. The resurrection of Jesus shows us that there is a vast difference between Christianity and all other religions. Whereas their founders are all dead (or dying) Jesus is eternally alive and, as we shall see later, confronts us in a way which radically affects us here and now — and will do so for ever. Nobody who thinks about it seriously can accept that Jesus is alive, shrug his or her shoulders and say, 'So what?'

9.
The greatest

Several years ago I met Muhammad Ali, the heavyweight boxing champion of the world. Mercifully, it was outside of the ring, and we traded words, not punches, but it was an interesting experience for all that. In his prime, Ali's trademark boast was, 'I am the greatest!' He probably believed it (and may have been right) and we can be sure that promoters made good use of his claim in pushing ticket sales.

Many people have made colossal claims about their strength, intelligence, wealth, ability, popularity or influence, and in many cases it has not been difficult to decide which were true and which were false.

One of the most remarkable things about Jesus is that he combined great humility with the most amazing claims any human being could possibly make. He never accumulated money, property or possessions, and wealth seemed to hold no attraction for him. He had to borrow a boat to get across the Sea of Galilee, a donkey to ride into Jerusalem and even a coin to give an illustration. As to his humility, he told his friends that he 'did not come to be served, but to serve'.[177] At a farewell meal with them, he demonstrated this by getting down on his hands and knees and washing their dusty feet, a common chore which everybody else seemed anxious to avoid.[178] Yet his claims were stupendous. Here are some of them:

1. *'I am the light of the world. Whoever follows me will never walk in darkness, but will have the light of life'*[179]

While other people groped and stumbled their way through life, trying to find an answer to its mysteries and conflicts, Jesus claimed that he, *and he alone*, could steer them in the right direction. There was no need for them to be blinded by moral and spiritual ignorance; Jesus could provide all the illumination they needed.

2. *'I am the bread of life. He who comes to me will never go hungry, and he who believes in me will never be thirsty'*[180]

Jesus was obviously not referring to any kind of life, but to the spiritual life which comes from a personal relationship with God. Thousands of people were trying to achieve this by their own religious and moral efforts; Jesus claimed that they would receive it only by putting their trust in him.

3. *'I am the way and the truth and the life. No one comes to the Father except through me'*[181]

The deepest spiritual longing of men and women was to find God and to know him as a dynamic reality in their lives; Jesus claimed that there was no other way of doing so except through him and that he was the true and living way to the life they sought.

4. 'I am the true vine ... apart from me you can do nothing'[182]

Surrounded by all kinds of moral and spiritual pressures, and betrayed by their own weaknesses, people were frustrated, restless and empty. They needed an inner strength in order to cope; Jesus claimed that they would be able to find it only with his help.

5. 'I am the resurrection and the life. He who believes in me will live, even though he dies; and whoever lives and believes in me will never die'[183]

The human spirit has always looked for existence beyond the few years we spend on this earth, and Old Testament writers had pointed to the possibility of eternal life in God's joyful presence. Jesus claimed that he alone could grant this. For those who believed in him, physical death would be the doorway into a dimension of life in which, as the Bible puts it, 'There will be no more death or mourning or crying or pain.'[184]

The big one

When these claims are added to his assertions that he was the fulfilment of all the Messianic prophecies, that he lived a sinless life, that he died to bear the punishment for other people's sins, that he rose again from the dead and that he is eternally alive, it can fairly be argued that nobody else (not even Muhammad Ali) is in the same league. Yet Jesus made another set of claims which went far beyond even these. Taken together, they amounted to this: *he claimed to be God*. Although he is never on record as using the phrase 'I am God', there are at least six instances in which he made the same stupendous claim using different words.

1. When nit-picking religionists complained about him healing a paralytic on the Sabbath day, Jesus replied, 'My Father is always at his work to this very day, and I, too, am working.'[185] That may seem an innocuous statement to us, but there is more to it than meets the modern eye. In the first place, Jesus was telling them that he was not bound by their legalistic interpretation of the Jewish law. Secondly, he claimed that he was doing exactly what God was doing. The Jews certainly had no doubts as to what he meant; he was 'making himself equal with God',[186] *and Jesus did nothing to correct their interpretation.*

2. In a discussion with the Jews about the Old Testament patriarch Abraham, Jesus replied to a question by stating, 'Before Abraham was born, I am!'[187] This was an unusual answer, to say the least, as they were not questioning him about his age, but about his identity: 'Are you *greater* than our father Abraham? ... Who do you think you are?'[188] But what makes the reply so stunning is

that 'I AM' was one of the names by which God revealed himself in the Old Testament. When giving Moses certain instructions for his people, God said, 'This is what you are to say to the Israelites: "I AM has sent me to you."'[189] 'I AM' is a title which speaks of absolute, timeless self-existence, qualities which can be true only of God, yet Jesus calmly used it about himself. Those listening to him had no doubts about what he meant; they immediately 'picked up stones to stone him',[190] a clear sign that they were accusing him of blasphemy. J. C. Ryle, the first Bishop of Liverpool, once said, 'All claims to evade this explanation appear to me to be so preposterous that it is a waste of time to notice them.'

3. At the end of one particular teaching session, Jesus suddenly stated, 'I and the Father are one.'[191] The crucial point here is that 'one' is not masculine, but neuter. Jesus was not claiming to be one in person with God, but one in essence or nature. Once more his enemies 'picked up stones to stone him',[192] and again made it clear why they did so. When Jesus asked them, 'I have shown you many great miracles from the Father. For which of these do you stone me?', they replied, 'We are not stoning you for any of these ... but for blasphemy, because you, a mere man, claim to be God.'[193] If this was a catastrophic mis-understanding on their part, *why did Jesus not correct them*?

4. When one of his disciples asked him, 'Lord, show us the Father and that will be enough for us,' Jesus replied,

'Don't you know me, Philip, even after I have been among you such a long time? Anyone who has seen me has seen the Father. How can you say, "Show us the Father"? Don't you believe that I am in the Father, and that the Father is in me?'[194] Jesus was not claiming to *be* the Father, but that in his own life and personality he was revealing all of God's nature and character that it was possible and necessary for any human being to know on this earth: it was a clear claim to deity.

5. A few hours before his death, Jesus prayed, 'And now, Father, glorify me in your presence with the glory I had with you before the world began.'[195] This speaks of Jesus resuming a heavenly status which he had possessed by divine right before time began. This is either blasphemous balderdash or it tells us that Jesus is addressing God on equal terms. In the light of what we have already discovered, is it difficult to decide between those alternatives?

6. The last of these claims was made when Jesus was arrested just before his execution. As the soldiers closed in, Jesus asked them, 'Who is it you want?' When they replied, 'Jesus of Nazareth', he told them, 'I am he.'[196] This seems perfectly straightforward, yet the soldiers' reaction was amazing: 'When Jesus said, "I am he," they drew back and fell to the ground.'[197] At that point, Jesus was offering no resistance and appeared helpless, yet an entire detachment of hand-picked soldiers collapsed in a heap. This would hardly qualify them for the commandos! How can we possibly explain their eccentric behaviour? The only credible answer seems to lie in the phrase

Jesus used to identify himself — *'ego eimi'* ('I am'). But why should four syllables flatten a squad of soldiers? There was apparently something about the majesty and glory of the words (the divine title he used in the second claim we looked at earlier), and the way in which they were spoken, which swept the troops to the ground in a spectacular demonstration of the presence and power of God.

In the musical *Jesus Christ Superstar* one of the cast sings, 'He's a man, he's just a man,' but it is impossible to square this with these six claims. Nor is there any way to deny that Jesus claimed to be more than even the greatest of men who ever lived. Nobody can get away with saying that, although he may have been a great teacher, his claim to be God was mistaken or false. C. S. Lewis easily torpedoed that idea: 'That is the one thing we must not say. A man who was merely a man and said the sort of things Jesus said would not be a great moral teacher. He would either be a lunatic — on a level with a man who says he is a poached egg — or else he would be the devil of hell. You must make your choice... You can shut him up for a fool, you can spit at him and kill him as a demon; or you can fall at his feet and call him Lord and God. But let us not come up with any patronizing nonsense about his being a great human teacher. *He has not left that open to us. He did not intend to.*'

Rhetoric or reality?

Jesus is far from being the only person in history who has claimed to be God. The leaders of many bizarre and discredited religions and cults have made claims to divinity: for example, the American actress Shirley MacLaine trumpeted her New Age ideas by standing on the shore of the Pacific Ocean shouting, 'I am God! I am God! I am God!' While such people have never been able to live up to their claims, exactly the opposite is true in Jesus' case, as we can easily confirm.

If God came to earth in human form, we would expect him to be utterly without sin of any kind, perfect in every way: *Jesus was*. He was 'holy, blameless, pure, set apart from sinners'.[198] We would expect him to be able to create anything he chose out of whatever materials were at his disposal: *Jesus was*. As a wedding guest, he rescued an embarrassing situation by turning water into the day's finest wine.[199] He once fed over 5,000 hungry people with a handful of bread and fish,[200] and on another occasion did the same thing for a crowd of over 4,000.[201] We would expect him to be in control of the natural elements: *Jesus was*. When a sudden storm threatened to sink his friends' boat, 'He got up and rebuked the wind and the waves, and it was completely calm.'[202] If he chose to do so, we should expect him to heal people who were sick: *Jesus did*. He healed the blind, the deaf, the dumb, the lame, the paralysed and those suffering from leprosy. The range of his healing miracles was so great that at one point we read of him curing 'every disease and sickness'.[203] Virtually all the healings were instantaneous, and there is no record of a single relapse. We would expect him to have power over demonic forces: *Jesus did*. We are told that he cast out evil spirits and healed 'all who were under the

power of the devil'.[204] We would expect him to be able to
raise the dead: *Jesus did*. He brought at least three people
back to life; a twelve-year old girl within an hour or two
of her death,[205] a man whose body was being carried to
the cemetery,[206] and another who had been buried four
days earlier.[207]

The famous nineteenth-century French artist Paul
Gustav Doré once lost his passport while he was abroad.
When he explained the situation at the next international
border, and assured the immigration officer that he *was*
Doré, the official handed him paper and pencil and said,
'Prove it!' Doré's brilliant sketch soon convinced the of-
ficial. The miracles of Jesus point to an infinitely greater
claim.

God's prerogatives

If actions are said to speak louder than words, these miracles say a great deal about Jesus' claim to be divine. Yet
the Bible tells us of even greater things Jesus did — things
which only God could possibly do. Five examples will be
sufficient to make the point.

1. Creation

The Bible's opening words are: 'In the beginning God
created the heavens and the earth.'[208] This is the most
fundamental of all God's works, bringing into being all
reality outside of himself, including time and space. Yet

the New Testament says of *Jesus*, that 'By him all things
were created: things in heaven and on earth, visible and
invisible, whether thrones or powers or rulers or authorities; all things were created by him and for him.'[209] There
is no way of avoiding what this is telling us. The same
Jesus who was born in Bethlehem as a helpless baby is
the Creator of the entire universe.

2. Preservation

When his original work of creation was complete, God
did not turn his back on it, like a groundsman marking
out a football pitch and then letting others get on with the
game. Instead, nature and all its laws are held in place by
God's sustaining power; in the Bible's words, 'The LORD
has established his throne in heaven, and his kingdom rules
over all.'[210] Yet the Bible specifically says that it is *Jesus*
who is 'sustaining all things by his powerful word'[211] and
that 'In him all things hold together.'[212] It is Jesus who
prevents our cosmos from becoming chaos. Every atom
in the universe is held together by 'his powerful word'.
Who but God could possibly do this?

3. Salvation

The Bible teaches that humankind is the crown of God's
creation and that no amount of wealth, fame, popularity,
ability or influence can make up for the absence of a living and eternal relationship with him. The Bible calls this
'salvation' and teaches that only God can bring it about.

The Old Testament speaks of 'God our Saviour'[213] and insists, 'The salvation of the righteous comes from the LORD.'[214] In the Old Testament, 'God' and 'Saviour' are virtually identical terms; in the New Testament, *Jesus* is said to be that Saviour. The very name 'Jesus' means 'Jehovah [God] is salvation'. We are told that Jesus 'came into the world to save sinners'.[215] What is more, he is the only Saviour possible: 'Salvation is found in no one else, for there is no other name under heaven given to men by which we must be saved.'[216] Salvation is an even greater work than creation, yet Jesus is said to be 'the Saviour of the world'.[217] What does that say about his identity?

4. The forgiveness of sins

We need to take a closer look at two particular aspects of salvation. The first is the forgiveness of sins. Guilt is one of man's greatest problems, and forgiveness one of his deepest needs, one which only God can meet. As the Old Testament makes clear, 'To the LORD our God belong compassion and forgiveness';[218] in other words, these are God's prerogatives. Yet *Jesus* claimed to forgive people's sins. Your reaction to this may be: 'But surely we are all meant to forgive other people. What is so remarkable about Jesus doing this?' The answer is not difficult to find.

When four men brought their paralysed friend to Jesus in the hope that he might heal him, the first thing Jesus said to him was: 'Son, your sins are forgiven.'[219] Do you see something unusual here? As far as we know, Jesus had never seen this man before and his offences had not been committed against Jesus as a fellow human being. Yet Jesus told him that his sins — *all of them* — were forgiven. The slate was wiped clean and the man could make a fresh start in life, without any sense of guilt or shame. But unless Jesus was more than a man, how could he possibly give him that kind of assurance? How could he forgive sins that appeared to be none of his business?

Let me illustrate. Imagine that you and I are together at a party in someone's house. As I leave for home, a £50 note drops out of my pocket. (This *is* just a story!) As you are short of ready cash, you decide to pocket the £50, but some weeks later your conscience begins to trouble you. When you share your problem with a friend, she says, 'Don't worry about it. John doesn't know you picked it up. I'll forgive you. Now forget about it.'

Do you sense something odd about this? Humanly speaking, *I* am the only person who can forgive you, because the offence was committed against *me*. Nobody else has the authority to forgive sins committed against a third party — and if you would introduce me to your generous friend, I would gently explain this to her!

Yet this is exactly what Jesus did, time after time. He behaved as if he were the person chiefly offended by all the offences concerned. Without ever consulting the injured parties, he told people that *all* their sins, even the most serious, regardless of how many there were and how long ago they had been committed, were completely forgiven, wiped out of existence. But this makes sense only if he really *was* the God whose laws are broken every time a sin is committed. The religious leaders listening to

Jesus realized this and at least got halfway to the truth: 'Why does this fellow talk like that? He's blaspheming! Who can forgive sins but God alone?'[220] They knew perfectly well that all sin was against God, who alone could remove the guilt and pardon the sinner. Their theology was right, but their conclusion was wrong. They missed the vital truth that was staring them in the face. We have no excuse for making the same mistake.

5. *Eternal life*

The second aspect of salvation we need to look at is eternal life, which begins on earth when a person gets right with God and continues for ever in heaven, 'the home of righteousness'.[221] As with forgiveness, it is obvious that only God has the authority and power to grant eternal life; as the Bible puts it, 'The LORD bestows his blessing, even life for evermore.'[222] Yet *Jesus* claimed this authority and ability, and assured his listeners, 'The Son ... gives life to whom he wishes.'[223] Later, he said of God's people, 'I give them eternal life, and they shall never perish; no one can snatch them out of my hand.'[224] The implication is obvious: if Jesus is not God, these words are religious claptrap. All the evidence suggests that he is — and that they are not.

Eloquent silence

In this chapter, we have only been able to scratch the surface of the Bible's witness to the deity of Jesus, but there is one other significant pointer I would like to add. This was the way in which Jesus sometimes emphasized his claim to be God *by doing nothing*.

The Bible tells us of two occasions when people were so impressed by the status or powers of the apostles that they treated them with exaggerated respect. In the first case, an angel appeared to a God-fearing Roman centurion by the name of Cornelius who was stationed at the Palestinian seaport of Caesarea, and told him to send for the apostle Peter, who was to bring him an important message about the spread of the Christian gospel among the Gentiles. When Peter arrived two days later, Cornelius was so overwhelmed that he 'fell at his feet in reverence'.[225] Most people have an appetite for appreciation and are happy to take all the acclaim they can get, but the apostle's reaction was very different: 'Peter made him get up. "Stand up," he said, "I am only a man myself."'[226] He wanted Cornelius to be clear that prostrating oneself before another human being in this way was totally out of place and that God alone was worthy of man's worship.

The second incident took place in the city of Lystra. When the apostle Paul healed a cripple, the people thought he and his companion Barnabas were pagan gods in human form and 'wanted to offer sacrifices to them'.[227] Their reaction was exactly the same as that of Peter to Cornelius: 'But when the apostles Barnabas and Paul heard of this, they tore their clothes [an expression of horror at the people's blasphemy] and rushed out into the crowd, shouting, "Men, why are you doing this? We too are only men, human like you. We are bringing you good news, telling you to turn from these worthless things to the living God."'[228]

Then how did Jesus react when people flung themselves at his feet and worshipped him? *He did nothing*! Although his whole life had been characterized by meekness and humility, he always accepted the worship of others as his due. The most striking example of this came after his resurrection. When the man we often call 'Doubting Thomas' was finally convinced that Jesus had been raised from the dead, he cried out, 'My Lord and my God![229] and *Jesus did nothing to rebuke or correct him*. To worship anyone but God is idolatry, and for anyone but God to accept worship is blasphemy. Can you hear what Jesus' silence is saying?

10.
The moment of truth

My thirteen years spent working in and around the law courts in Guernsey sharpened my understanding that in any civil or criminal action the one moment that ultimately matters is the one in which the court announces its decision. We have reached a similar position in this book.

We began by asking, 'What is the millennium all about?', and discovered that it hinges on Jesus of Nazareth, who reset the clocks of history when he was born in Bethlehem roughly 2,000 years ago. The more we discovered about him, the clearer it became that he was no ordinary person. His conception, character, words and deeds showed him to stand head and shoulders above every one of the sixty billion other human beings who have ever inhabited our planet, before or after 'day zero'.

Yet the issue that eventually demands a response is not the circumstances surrounding his birth, nor the authority of his teaching, nor the meaning of his miracles, nor the way he died, nor the extraordinary business of his resurrection. Each of these has a bearing on the case, but the ultimate question is this: *who is he*? There are just four possibilities.

1. Was he evil?

Some would claim that, just like other people, *he was a sinner*. In particular, they would say that he was being malicious when he claimed to fulfil Old Testament prophecy, when he taught that he alone was the answer to people's moral and spiritual needs and when he claimed to forgive sins and grant eternal life. These are serious charges. In the first place, they imply that he was a blasphemous liar; he knew perfectly well that he was not divine, yet, like the leader of some bizarre cult, he tried to trick people into believing that he was. They also mean that he was a wicked deceiver. All around him people were 'harassed and helpless, like sheep without a shepherd',[230] crushed under a tangled mass of religious rules and regulations. By pretending that he, and he alone, could remove this burden and meet their deepest spiritual needs, he was showing himself to be not only wicked but callous and cruel. To cap it all, he was a hypocrite, preaching one thing and practising another. He taught honesty, yet constantly lied about his own identity and ability; he taught humility, yet arrogantly accepted other people's worship.

Anybody guilty of such wholesale lying, blasphemy, deceit and hypocrisy would certainly have been evil beyond words, but does this verdict square with the character we see on the pages of Scripture? Here we find someone who is loving, gracious, compassionate, gentle and sympathetic, and who has all these virtues in perfect balance and under total control — hardly the hallmarks of someone who is demonically evil. What is more, if Jesus was so thoroughly evil, how do we explain his amazing and unique influence for good over the last 2,000 years? The nineteenth-century American scholar Phillips Brooks was not exaggerating when he wrote, 'All the armies that ever marched, and all the navies that ever were built, and all the parliaments that ever sat, and all the kings that ever reigned, put together, have not affected the life of man upon this earth as powerfully as has this one solitary life — the life of Jesus Christ.' Many of the greatest moral revolutions in history have been triggered by pioneers who were inspired by his example and teaching, and today countless millions of men and women all around the world claim that he has brought moral and spiritual revolution to their lives. How can we explain this if Jesus was rotten to the core?

2. Was he labouring under a delusion?

The second option is to say that *he was deluded about his own identity*. Simply put, this means that his moral teaching was fine, and might even have been the finest the world has ever seen but, like so many exceptional characters in history, he had a fundamental flaw. In his case, it was a strange obsession with the idea that he was not merely a great man, but God himself in human form.

This sounds like a more promising approach, as it allows us to deny his deity without casting aspersions on his character or his teaching. But this is easier said than done, because his character and his claims were all of a piece. For example, he repeatedly endorsed Old Testament teaching, but also said, 'These are the Scriptures that

testify about *me*.'[231] Again, he spoke not only of 'the kingdom of God',[232] but of '*my* kingdom'[233] and clearly in-
ferred that they were identical. As Kenneth Scott
Latourette says, 'It must be obvious to any thoughtful
reader of the Gospels that Jesus regarded his message
and himself as inseparable. He was a great teacher, but he
was more. His teaching about the kingdom of God, about
human conduct, and about God were important, but they
could not be divorced from him without, from his stand-
point, being vitiated [nullified].' In other words, if you
take away the things that Jesus said about himself, directly or indirectly, his teaching loses most of its impact.
His moral principles were based on his theology, and there
is no way in which we can prise them apart. To regard
him as a great moral teacher who was deluded about the
whole basis of his teaching is not difficult; it is impossible.

3. Was he insane?

The third option is to say that *he was mentally deranged*.
Insanity is a tragic condition, and religious mania has often
led to claims ranging from the humorous to the horrify-
ing, and to all kinds of irrational words and deeds.

Yet is this what we find when we read the Bible's account of Jesus? Is this man, whom we see healing the
sick, feeding the hungry, encouraging the sad, calming
the confused and comforting the bereaved, a lunatic? Far
from being unhinged, eccentric and self-centred, we find
him composed, balanced and constantly concerned with
the needs of others. As Bernard Palmer diagnoses, 'There

are no violent mood swings, depressive episodes or the schizophrenic's tendency to be out of touch with reality.' What about his teaching? Is the Lord's Prayer the product of a disturbed mind? Is the Sermon on the Mount an expression of insanity? Would a raving megalomaniac teach others to love their enemies, pray for their persecutors, give to the needy and turn their backs on materialism and immorality — and then set a perfect example of how to do these things? If this is insanity in practice, we urgently need a global epidemic of it! Those who assess the character of Jesus, listen to his words, look at what he did and then conclude that he is a maniac are telling us nothing about Jesus but a great deal about themselves.

4. Or was he God?

This eliminates three of the only four possible verdicts and leaves just one: *Jesus is God*. Everything points in that direction and none of the three alternatives fits the facts. The issue is not merely beyond reasonable doubt, but beyond doubt of any kind. The weight and consistency of the evidence are overwhelming, and for nearly 2,000 years it has remained without a successful challenge.

Why bother?

You may already have come to this conclusion, or be in the process of coming to it as you move towards the end of this book. On the other hand, you may still be undecided, or be wondering why you should feel under any obligation to make up your mind one way or the other. As far as being undecided is concerned, Jesus ruled this out: 'He who is not with me is against me.'[234] Sitting on the fence may be sensible on some issues, but it is impossible on this one, for the simple reason that there is no fence on which to sit. God has spoken so clearly and consistently that the person who hesitates to accept what he has said is in effect rejecting his testimony. On this issue, at least, there is no room for neutrality.

But is there any personal need to decide one way or the other? After all, there is no such pressure on judges, magistrates and jurors, who act on behalf of the state or some other authority. They are not personally involved in the case before them and are not normally affected by the outcome. But Jesus himself made it clear that a verdict on his identity is a different matter altogether: '*If you do not believe that I am the one I claim to be, you will ... die in your sins.*'[235] The destiny on the line here is not his, but ours.

Do you see why this statement applies to you? The Bible says that 'All have sinned and fall short of the glory of God,'[236] and that 'The wages of sin is death.'[237] Whether they sense it or not, sinners are in desperate need, exposed to God's righteous anger and facing a day of final judgement when they will be 'punished with everlasting destruction and shut out from the presence of the Lord and from the majesty of his power'.[238] Nor is this fate reserved for those guilty of what might be thought of as the grossest sins. God's law is a unity, not a collection of bits and pieces, and 'Whoever keeps the whole law and yet stumbles at just one point is guilty of breaking all of it.'[239] Just as snapping one link severs an entire chain, so one sin is sufficient to break the whole of God's law. *Now* where do you stand? You may have avoided murder, rape, child abuse or robbery with violence, but what about sins such as pride, dishonesty, envy, greed, selfishness, covetousness, jealousy and blasphemy?

What about the things you have *failed* to do? Those who hope to get right with God by their own efforts have missed the point that anyone 'who knows the good he ought to do and doesn't do it, sins'.[240] Have you *always* done *all* the good you possibly could? It is one thing to claim, as many do, that you try to live by the so-called 'Golden Rule' — 'In everything, do to others what you would have them do to you'[241] — but the question is not whether you try but whether you succeed! As we have just seen, failing to keep God's law in *every* part is to be guilty of 'breaking all of it'. To rely on your own moral or spiritual performance is fatal.

Nor is this the worst fact to be faced. When a religious expert asked him which was the most important of the Ten Commandments, Jesus gave him this brilliant summary of the first four: 'Love the Lord your God with all your heart and with all your soul and with all your mind and with all your strength.'[242] Can you honestly claim to have done that — and to be doing it now? If not, then far from making what you might think is a pretty good attempt at keeping at least some of the Ten Commandments, you are constantly breaking what Jesus called 'the most important one'.[243] Then how can you ever hope to get right with God under your own steam?

This brings us back to your verdict on Jesus, which is the clinching issue. To deny his divinity is to disagree with God about the identity of 'his only begotten Son'[244] by rejecting his testimony that in Jesus 'all the fulness of the Deity lives in bodily form'.[245] As this amounts to calling God a liar, we should not be surprised to read that the issue is literally a matter of spiritual life and death: 'Whoever believes in [God's Son] is not condemned, but whoever does not believe stands condemned already because he has not believed in the name of God's one and only Son.'[246] It is impossible to avoid the Bible's insistence that your response to the divinity of Jesus is the issue on which your eternal destiny hangs. Can you afford to be undecided or indifferent about it?

Look at it from another angle. Imagine that you arrange a lavish party to celebrate a special birthday. The big day arrives and the guests are making hilarious inroads into the food and drink you have generously provided when you notice something very disturbing. Although there are piles of cards and presents, not one has your name on it! To make matters worse, the guests are totally ignoring you while enjoying each other's company. Would you not think their behaviour ungrateful, self-centred and shameful? Then what do you say of those who turn their backs on the one who provides all their needs and who paid such a terrible price to save sinners from the punishment they deserve?

Believing and believing

As this book ends, one vitally important thing needs to be added. When the Bible speaks about 'believing' in Jesus, it uses the word in a very specific way. The word literally means 'trusting', something involving not merely the mind, but also the heart and the will. Believing in Jesus Christ means much more than accepting that what the Bible says about him is true. Jesus is not a logical proposition but a living person, and he demands a response which goes far beyond giving your endorsement to a list of facts about him.

- It means acknowledging that you are a sinner by nature and by choice, and that you are unable to do anything to earn God's favour. It also involves a whole-hearted longing to turn from sin and to live in a way that is pleasing to God.
- It means truly believing that when Jesus died in the place of sinners he did so *in their place and on their behalf.* Having believed in this way, the apostle Paul was able to speak of Jesus as 'the Son of God, who loved *me* and gave himself for *me*'.[247] Trusting him like this implies turning away from trusting in anything or anyone else for salvation. Jesus is not merely the *only* Saviour of sinners, he is the *exclusive* Saviour, and you must trust him exclusively.
- It means whole-hearted commitment to Jesus as the one who rose again from the dead, is eternally alive, and has the prior claim on your heart and life. The Bible makes

it clear that those for whom Jesus died 'should no longer live for themselves but for him who died for them and was raised again'.[248] Believing in Jesus Christ (in other words, becoming a true Christian) means more than confessing your sins and calling upon him to have mercy on you. It means abandoning your self-centred independence and submitting to him as your rightful Lord. As a friend of mine once put it, the whole of your life must be on an 'open palm', so that Jesus can take away whatever he wants to whenever he wants to, and give you whatever he wants whenever he wants to. This may sound daunting, risky and restricting, but it is exactly the opposite. Jesus never impoverishes people's lives; he enriches them, promising life 'to the full'.[249] Millions of people all over the world testify that he keeps that promise.

He keeps *all* of his promises. Peace with God, help in resisting temptation, spiritual wisdom when facing tough choices, strength to get you through the difficult times and, at the end of this life, an eternal home in heaven, where there will be 'no more death or mourning or crying or pain'.[250] are some of 'his very great and precious promises',[251] and he makes them to all who trust him as their Saviour and take him as their Lord.

Can you think of any good reason to turn them aside, to refuse his gracious invitation and to reject his amazing love? The Bible makes it clear what your response should be:

Seek the LORD while he may be found;
    call on him while he is near.

Let the wicked forsake his way
   and the evil man his thoughts.
Let him turn to the LORD, and he will have mercy
      on him,
   and to our God, for he will freely pardon. [252]

The best place to take God at his word is right where
you are.

The best time to do so is *now*.

Postscript

If you have come to acknowledge Jesus Christ as your Saviour and Lord as a result of reading this book, and would like help in understanding the Bible, you are invited to write for a free copy of *Read Mark Learn*, John Blanchard's book of guidelines for personal Bible study. Write to:

John Blanchard
c/o Evangelical Press
Grange Close
Faverdale North Industrial Estate
Darlington
DL3 OPH
England

Bible references

All quotations from the Bible have been numbered and can be found at the places indicated below. References marked with a single asterisk (*) are from the New American Standard Bible and the one marked with a double asterisk (**) is from the Amplified Bible. All other references are from the New International Version.

1. 2 Peter 1:21
2. 1 Peter 1:23
3. John 7:12
4. John 7:43
5. John 9:16
6. See Matthew 16:14
7. See Matthew 9:34
8. John 10:20
9. Luke 7:34
10. See Matthew 26:65
11. See John 9:16
12. See Matthew 11:19
13. See John 19:12
14. Luke 2:7
15. See Luke 2:21
16. Luke 2:16
17. Luke 2:27
18. Luke 2:43
19. See Matthew 21:18
20. See John 4:7
21. John 4:6
22. See Matthew 8:24
23. See Luke 23:26
24. John 19:34
25. Luke 2:52
26. Mark 6:38
27. Mark 9:21
28. John 11:34
29. John 15:15
30. John 11:5
31. Mark 10:14
32. Luke 13:32
33. Matthew 7:15
34. Matthew 23:33
35. Matthew 23:17
36. Matthew 23:27
37. Matthew 23:29
38. See Matthew 21:12-13
39. Luke 19:41
40. Mark 7:34
41. Matthew 9:36
42. Luke 10:21

43.	Hebrews 4:15	81.	Hebrews 7:26
44.	Luke 4:16	82.	Hebrews 9:14
45.	Acts 2:43	83.	2 Corinthians 11:23
46.	Acts 8:6	84.	1 Peter 1:19
47.	Luke 1:26-38	85.	1 Peter 2:22
48.	Matthew 1:18-21	86.	e.g. John 21:7
49.	Matthew 1:24-25	87.	1 John 3:3
50.	See Mark 6:3	88.	1 John 3:7
51.	See Deuteronomy 7:6	89.	1 John 3:5
52.	Malachi 3:1	90.	2 Samuel 24:10
53.	Luke 4:18-19	91.	Isaiah 6:5
54.	Luke 4:20-21	92.	Job 42:6
55.	John 5:39-40	93.	1 John 1:8
56.	John 15:25	94.	John 8:29
57.	John 5:46	95.	Matthew 7:11
58.	Daniel 7:13	96.	Matthew 6:12
59.	See e.g. Matthew 9:6	97.	Matthew 6:9
60.	Genesis 22:18	98.	John 14:30
61.	Jeremiah 23:5	99.	Luke 3:22
62.	Genesis 49:10	100.	Matthew 17:5
63.	Micah 5:2	101.	Romans 3:23
64.	Matthew 2:1	102.	Matthew 21:13
65.	Isaiah 7:14	103.	Ephesians 4:26*
66.	See Joel 1:8	104.	Psalm 7:11
67.	1 Peter 2:21	105.	Matthew 21:18-19
68.	John 8:50	106.	Matthew 21:43
69.	Luke 22:27	107.	Mark 10:17-18
70.	Matthew 11:29	108.	Mark 10:19
71.	Hebrews 4:15	109.	Mark 10:20
72.	John 18:38	110.	Mark 10:22
73.	Matthew 27:19	111.	Exodus 20:3
74.	Matthew 27:3-4	112.	John 8:46
75.	Luke 23:39	113.	See Deuteronomy 21:23
76.	Luke 23:40-41	114.	1 Corinthians 1:23**
77.	Luke 23:47	115.	1 Corinthians 1:23
78.	Acts 9:1	116.	1 Corinthians 2:2
79.	Acts 9:2	117.	John 2:4
80.	2 Corinthians 5:21	118.	John 7:30; 8:20

119.   John 12:23,27
120.   John 17:1
121.   Genesis 1:27
122.   Genesis 2:17
123.   Genesis 5:3
124.   Matthew 15:19
125.   Romans 8:2
126.   Hebrews 9:27
127.   John 10:18
128.   Matthew 26:53
129.   Matthew 27:50
130.   Ecclesiastes 8:8
131.   See Matthew 27:34
132.   Matthew 27:50
133.   Luke 22:37
134.   Matthew 26:28
135.   Romans 5:6
136.   Romans 5:8
137.   1 Peter 2:24
138.   1 John 3:16
139.   Luke 9:31*
140.   John 19:30
141.   1 John 2:2
142.   Mark 10:45
143.   Romans 6:6
144.   Romans 5:10
145.   Romans 5:1
146.   1 Peter 3:18*
147.   Matthew 27:63
148.   Matthew 27:65
149.   Acts 2:23*
150.   Mark 15:47
151.   Luke 23:55
152.   See Matthew 28:2-4
153.   Matthew 28:12-14
154.   John 20:19
155.   1 Corinthians 15:15*
156.   Acts 5:29

157.   See John 19:34
158.   See John 20:10-18
159.   John 20:14-18; Matthew 28:8-9
160.   1 Corinthians 15:7 (see John 7:5; Gal. 1:19)
161.   John 21:1-14
162.   1 Corinthians 15:8
163.   John 20:24-28
164.   1 Corinthians 15:6
165.   See Mark 16:1
166.   Matthew 28:9
167.   Luke 24:30
168.   Acts 10:41
169.   See John 20:25
170.   John 20:27
171.   See Matthew 26:69-70
172.   Acts 4:13
173.   Acts 17:6
174.   Acts 2:32
175.   Acts 4:10
176.   1 Corinthians 15:4
177.   Matthew 20:28
178.   See John 13:1-17
179.   John 8:12
180.   John 6:35
181.   John 14:6
182.   John 15:1-5
183.   John 11:25
184.   Revelation 21:4
185.   John 5:17
186.   John 5:18
187.   John 8:58
188.   John 8:53
189.   Exodus 3:14
190.   John 8:59
191.   John 10:30
192.   John 10:31

193. John 10:32,33
194. John 14:8-10
195. John 17:5
196. John 18:4,5
197. John 18:6
198. Hebrews 7:26
199. See John 2:1-11
200. See Matthew 14:13-21
201. See Matthew 15:29-38
202. Matthew 8:26
203. Matthew 9:35
204. Acts 10:38
205. See Mark 5:21-43
206. See Luke 7:11-17
207. See John 11:1-44
208. Genesis 1:1
209. Colossians 1:16
210. Psalm 103:19
211. Hebrews 1:3
212. Colossians 1:17
213. Psalm 68:19
214. Psalm 37:39
215. 1 Timothy 1:15
216. Acts 4:12
217. 1 John 4:14
218. Daniel 9:9*
219. Mark 2:5
220. Mark 2:7
221. 2 Peter 3:13
222. Psalm 133:3

223. John 5:21*
224. John 10:28
225. Acts 10:25
226. Acts 10:26
227. Acts 14:13
228. Acts 14:14-15
229. John 20:28
230. Matthew 9:36
231. John 5:39
232. Luke 10:9
233. John 18:36
234. Luke 11:23
235. John 8:24
236. Romans 3:23
237. Romans 6:23
238. 2 Thessalonians 1:9
239. James 2:10
240. James 4:17
241. Matthew 7:12
242. Mark 12:30
243. Mark 12:29
244. John 3:16*
245. Colossians 2:9
246. John 3:18
247. Galatians 2:20
248. 2 Corinthians 5:15
249. John 10:10
250. Revelation 21:4
251. 2 Peter 1:4
252. Isaiah 55:6-7

Scripture index